the making of modern london *1945–1985*

Steve Humphries and John Taylor

Sidgwick & Jackson
London

Photographs and illustrations were supplied or are reproduced by kind permission of the following: Jack Ailsby, 23; BBC Hulton Picture Library, 1, 4, 5, 13, 33, 52, 53, 64 (left), 68, 76, (left), 109, 113 (right), 127 (left), 131, 143; British Aerospace, 8, Camera Press, 20 (left), Charles Milligan, 106 (left), 121; Roy and Myrtle Campbell, 133; Jim and Dolly Cattle, 149; Central Press Photos Ltd, 20 (right), 58, 127 (right), 129 (right), 140; Colorific Picture Library, 37; Terence Conran, 50, 51; Tom Cook, 72; Margaret Dent, 57; Ford Motor Co., 11; Fox Photos Ltd, 76 (right), 102 (B. Waite), 145, 152 (left); Elsie Friday, 93; Greater London Council Archives, 141, 146, 147, 154; *Good Housekeeping* Magazine, 151 (bottom left); Harlow Council, 79, 89 (right), 91; Billy Kay, 31, 33 (right), 128 (left); Frederick Valerie Keeble, 96; Keystone Press Agency, 64 (right), 94, 106, 120, 122, 139, 152, 157, 159; Rose and Ron Linford 6 (right), 8 (right), 12; Alf and Anne Luhman, 87; Sheung Tang Mann: 128 (right); Mary Quant, 42; Eileen Murphy, 162; New Ideal Homes, 104; Photo Source, 113, 117; Prudential Assurance Co. Ltd, 56; Mr Raymond, 28; Rex Features Ltd, 44, 45; Ken Risby, 6 (left); Harley Sherlock, 151 (top left and right); Stevenage County Library, 89 (left); Stevenage Museum, 80, 83, 84, 90; Sun Alliance, 65; Syndication International, 71; Topham Picture Library, 26, 30, 35, 42; Alan Townsin, 9, 42

First published in Great Britain in 1986
by Sidgwick and Jackson Limited

Picture research by Katrina Ure and Linda Stradling

Designed by Type Generation
ISBN 0-283–99368-5 (hardcover)
ISBN 0-283-99369-3 (softcover)

Typeset by Rapidset & Design Limited, London WC1
Printed and bound in Great Britain by
Biddles Ltd, Guildford, Surrey
for Sidgwick & Jackson Limited
1 Tavistock Chambers, Bloomsbury Way
London WC1A 2SG

Contents

Acknowledgements

We should like to thank everyone who has helped in the making of this book. For help with interviewees, information and our interpretation of post-war London history we are indebted to Stephen Potter and Ray Thomas of the Open University, Robin Oakley of Brunel University, Colin Ward, Alan Townsin, Christopher Booker, Don Hills of Stevenage Borough Council, Mandy Ashworth of Oxford House History Project, Ylva French of the London Visitor and Convention Bureau, Peter Daniels of the University of Liverpool, Simon Leonard and John Keefe of the GLC, Neil Killinbach of Islington Council Press Office, Barbara Dinham of the Transnational Information Centre, Richard Barrass, Leith Perry, Rodney Mace of the London History Centre, Raph Samuel of Ruskin College Oxford, Tricia Adams, Peter Hall of the University of Reading, Howard Bloch of Newham Libraries, Dennis Hardey and Judy Attfield of Middlesex Polytechnic, Rosemary Crompton of the University of East Anglia, David Hill and Ian Handy of the Sun Alliance Insurance Company, Chris Ellmers of the Museum of London, Mel Wright, Chris Denver of the GLC Archives, Elizabeth Davies of Stevenage Museum, Oliver Green of the London Transport Museum, John Slaughter of Islington Tenants' Association, Jackie Wadeson of *Hair and Beauty* Magazine, George Melly and Mary Cosh of the Islington Society.

We are also indebted to our colleagues at LWT for much advice, assistance and encouragement. Special thanks to Gavin Weightman, Mike Chaplin, Jane Hewland, Joanna Mack, Steve Schifferes and Pat Newbert. Sarah Adair, Anne Cornell and Mark Noades in the LWT library have again helped us a great deal, as has Derek Murgett and the LWT Photographic Department. Our production secretary and picture researcher, Linda Stradling, has made an enormous contribution, seeing the project through from the first outline to the finished product. Her tireless work and organizational skill have more than anything else made this book possible.

Finally, thanks to all the newspapers – too numerous to mention – who printed our appeals for memories; to Carey Smith and Katrina Ure for their help with the book; to Jack Rose; and last but not least a big thank you to everyone we interviewed for sharing their memories with us.

CHAPTER 1
Imperial Sunset

After the Second World War London was, in terms of wealth, and political and military influence, one of the greatest cities in the world. The Union Jack still flew over a quarter of the world's population, and many of these peoples looked to London as the centre of their government and trade. London was studded with monuments to the Empire and Commonwealth which had made it so rich and powerful. Towering warehouses hugged the docks and riverside, forming the world's largest emporium of goods in everything from exotic shells and ivory to bulk cargoes of tea and grain. The very names of many concerns, like Imperial Chemical Industries, the Plantation House Commodity Exchange and the Empire Mill in Victoria Dock, announced a strong imperial connection. And there were the famous landmarks of the Bank of England, Buckingham Palace, The Houses of Parliament and Whitehall. Inside the corridors of these buildings enormous international power was wielded. Most of these great edifices remain, of course, but their imperial heyday, when London's influence and domination extended throughout the world, is over. Forty years ago, however, most Londoners could see no reason why, having won the war, this power and prosperity should not continue indefinitely into the future. And after the lean austerity years this faith in Empire and Commonwealth seemed to be confirmed as London embarked on the glittering imperial ritual of the Coronation of Queen Elizabeth II.

On 2 June 1953 a million people lined the seven-mile route of the Coronation procession which went from Westminster Abbey to Buckingham Palace via the West End. Many, like Londoner Dolly Hyne, then aged fifteen, had camped out all night to make sure of the best views:

> Myself and my sister got down to Whitehall at about four o'clock in the afternoon on the day before the Coronation to make sure we got a good view. We decided we were going to sleep out and settled down on the pavement on a doormat with a rubberized bottom. But, as the night went on, the rain started to pour down and we were totally unprepared for it. We wrapped ourselves in my sister's bicycle cape, and all you could see were two little heads sticking out of the top of it. We

Previous page: Commonwealth troops parade down the Mall, forming part of the Coronation procession from Westminster Abbey to Buckingham Palace, June 1953. The procession – the greatest London had ever seen – was a remarkable testimony to London's continuing position as a world capital

> both got soaking wet; we were freezing cold and we had nothing to eat. By the time the morning came we were tired out and needed a couple of matches to keep our eyes open.

The procession – the greatest that London had ever seen – was a remarkable testimony to London's continuing position as a world capital. The leaders of over forty Commonwealth and Empire countries paraded in horse-drawn coaches, some of them, like the traditionally dressed Queen of Tonga from the South Sea Islands, creating a great impression. The march past was a showcase of military and civil power drawn from all over the Commonwealth. In it were 13,000 troops and 500 armed police, including colourful names like the New Guinea Constabulary, the Royal Canadian Mounted Police and the Papuans, who marched bare-legged and without hats as part of the Australian contingent. The entire cavalcade took forty-five minutes to pass any given point along the route.

To cap it all, on the very day the second Elizabethan age began it was announced that a Commonwealth team of climbers had, for the first time ever, scaled Mount Everest, the world's highest mountain. The timing of this had been carefully stage-managed to coincide with the Coronation, just as the Royal pageant, down to the last satin train, had itself been elaborately planned many months in advance.

Despite the fact that the weather – the one thing beyond the control of the organizers – let the side down (it poured with rain for most of the day), this extravagant piece of theatre had the desired effect of striking a deep patriotic and imperial chord amongst the new Queen's subjects.

The Coronation was followed by street parties all over the capital celebrating the new reign. The parties were reminiscent of those on VE-Day, but now the horrors of the war were just a memory for many Londoners and the worst years of rationing were behind them. This was a day of optimism when everyone looked forward to a better world. In the East End, for example, Ron and Rose Linford, who both worked at the Tate & Lyle sugar refinery, spent many weeks helping to organize the party in Maybury Road, Plaistow. Ron Linford remembers:

> At the time the Coronation was announced our street formed a committee and we held raffles to collect money for our party. Really, it was for the kids; we wanted to give them a day to remember. We bought toys and Coronation cups and mugs as presents for them. The women in the street did most of the work

Children prepare to eat delicacies like meat paste sandwiches, jelly and ice cream at the Morpeth Street Coronation party in the East End. This party, like most others, was staged on the weekend following the Coronation day, so that fathers and working mothers could attend

– they made all the flags and bunting out of crêpe paper. We put tables down the middle of the street and laid on ham sandwiches, and jelly and custard for the kids. There was lots of children's games, and races for the adults. It was a great day, you felt like you were coming out of the doldrums.

Rose Linford:

You felt as if something had been lifted and you could go out and be cheerful. During the war years everything had been dreary. Then there was rationing and we'd been short of things we wanted. But after the Coronation you had a great feeling that you had something wonderful to look forward to and you'd be able to have a bit more enjoyment.

In this book we look at what the new Elizabethan era in fact brought for Londoners and how life in the capital has changed in the forty years since the war. We begin by telling the story of how London's power as a world capital of trade and industry reached its zenith in the 1950s. But what looked like the dawning of a new age of prosperity for London industry proved in the long run to be the end of the old imperial era.

London had always been the hub of Empire and Commonwealth trade, and had grown fat on its wealth. For centuries much of the world's tea, coffee, wool, spices and many other products, had been shipped to London, stored in warehouses, sold on the exchanges, then shipped back to whatever country was buying the goods. This was called London's entrepôt trade.

After the Second World War trade with the Commonwealth increased even more, and throughout the 1950s it was at its highest ever level, accounting for around half of the Port of London's imports and exports. This flowering of Commonwealth trade was largely due to the Commonwealth Preference System, established in the early 1930s, which allowed free trade within the Commonwealth and erected high tariff barriers to discourage trade with other countries. The great advantage of Commonwealth trade for London was that it provided an endless supply of very cheap food and raw materials. By the mid-1950s almost a third of the total exports of all the Commonwealth countries was arriving in London: tea from India, wool and butter from Australia, wheat and timber from Canada, copper and gold from South Africa, and sugar from the Caribbean. Appropriately, Silvertown Way in Newham, East London, was still known as the 'road to Empire'.

This post-war resurgence of Commonwealth trade meant that many docks and wharfs in the Port of London were busier than they had ever been before. Almost every year in the 1950s a new record was set for the amounts of tonnage handled. In 1956 the Port handled a record 70 million tons of goods, which were transported in an average of 1000 ships that docked each week. Because the Commonwealth countries were historically united in their use of the sterling currency, buying and selling on London's commodity markets was often more straightforward than elsewhere. Thus in the mid-1950s London's position as a leading world port and market place seemed unassailable.

At this time there were around 30,000 men employed in the Port of London as dockers, stevedores, carters, clerks, crane operators, warehousemen and so on. One of the most skilled crafts was that of the lightermen, who ferried goods by barge or tug from

Lightermen, who ferried cargoes around the docks, enjoyed one of the most highly skilled and well-paid jobs on the riverside. After the war more than 7000 were employed in this occupation

ship to shore, from ship to ship, or from the main docks to the many small riverside wharfs and warehouses. There were about 7000 lightermen operating in the Port of London at this time, one of whom was Ken Rigby:

> In those days the river used to be so packed with ships and tugs and barges that you would often get the odd minor collision, especially with the barges under oars. When that happened you'd ship your oars, lie on the deck and hang on to something solid, to prevent being knocked over the side. We handled all sorts of cargoes from the Empire and Commonwealth trade. One of the most unusual I remember was large sacks of animal bones from North Africa. They were sent up to the mills at Bow on the River Lea and crushed for fertilizer. Bags would often burst – and you'd see camel jaws sticking out and they used to stink and have lots of green beetles all over them.

Most of the incoming goods would be processed or manufactured in some way rather than being simply re-exported in raw form. Processing and manufacturing was done in the rows of flour mills, breweries, refineries, sawmills, furniture and food factories which lined the riverside.

Below: Ken Rigby (far left) completed his apprenticeship as a lighterman in the early 1950s

Right: The Tate & Lyle Sugar refinery at Plaistow Wharf, in 1953. Tate & Lyle were the biggest sugar refiners not only in London but in the world

The classic 'post-imperial' food-processing industry in London was sugar-refining. This industry was dominated by Tate & Lyle, who had major factories in the East End on the riverside. They were the biggest sugar-refiners not only in London but in the world. After the war they successfully defeated plans by the Labour government to nationalize them by fighting a propaganda war, using the cartoon figure of Mr Cube (who still appears on the side of every bag of Tate & Lyle sugar). Mr Cube appeared in many newspapers, publicizing the virtues of free enterprise and the evils of state control, and by the mid-1950s Tate & Lyle were reaping the rewards of their campaign to remain a private company. At this time they employed almost 8000 in the capital and owned a fleet of ships as well.

But the prosperity of Tate & Lyle – like many other London food factories that depended on imports from new Commonwealth countries – was rooted in a plantation economy that was the legacy of the British Empire. Slavery had been finally abolished in early Victorian times, but the relationships of economic dependency it had engendered remained very strong in the 1950s. At this time Tate & Lyle owned plantations all over the Third World, a number of them in the West Indies.

The way in which the trade was made to revolve around London was quite remarkable. The cane was chopped, cleaned and boiled in factories on each plantation to produce raw sugar. Then this raw sugar was transported thousands of miles to Tate & Lyle's London factories, where it passed through a sophisticated refining process to produce granulated sugar. This then was shipped out again in millions of bags to countries all over the world, some of which had grown the sugar in the first place. By the mid-1950s a record 800,000 tons of sugar – half the total sugar refined – was exported, much of it to the Middle East, Africa and India. The rest of the sugar was sold in Britain, some of it as golden syrup or sugar cubes.

However, far and away the most important type of export from London to the Commonwealth was not processed food but manufactured goods – especially goods associated with the electrical and engineering industries. Traditionally, London had made and exported to the Commonwealth everything from lathes to lorries – goods which less-developed countries did not have the technology or know-how to produce. This supremacy was boosted even more in the inter-war years by the boom in electrical industries in West London which produced many new consumer items, like Osram lights and Belling cookers. This industrial base was strengthened during the war years when the production of aircraft, tanks

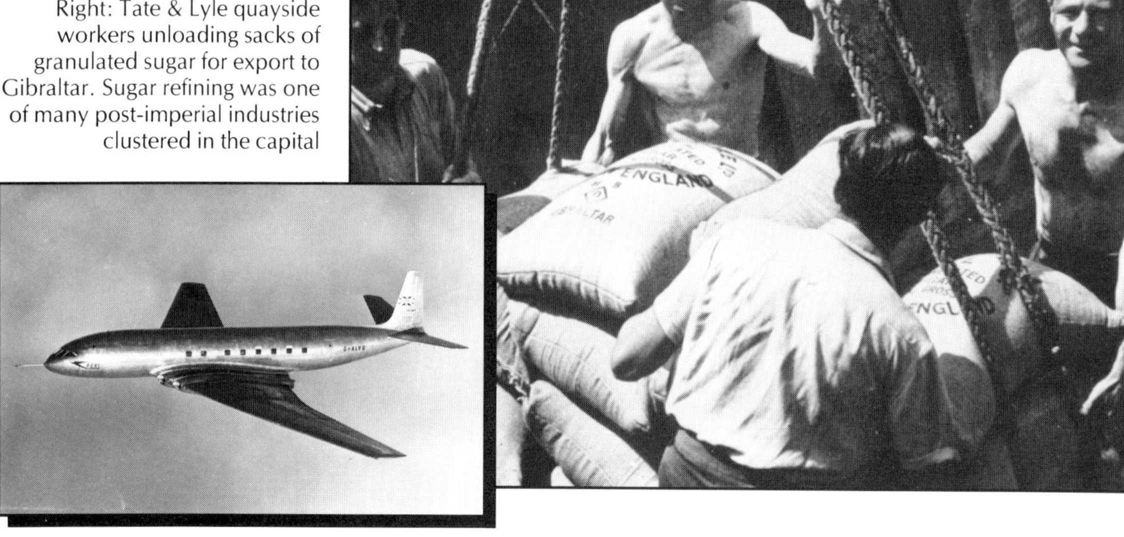

Right: Tate & Lyle quayside workers unloading sacks of granulated sugar for export to Gibraltar. Sugar refining was one of many post-imperial industries clustered in the capital

Above: One of the first test flights of the prototype Comet (Series 1) from Hatfield in 1949. The Comet won the race to produce the world's first jet airliner

and other weapons was concentrated in the capital. In peace-time London was to apply much of this new technology to the new growth in travel by air and road.

In the early 1950s London's aircraft industry reached unprecedented heights of power and prosperity. This was principally a consequence of generous financial backing from the government, which aimed to combat fierce competition from America and ensure that British planes would fly the Empire and European routes operated by the airlines BOAC and BEA. Also it wanted planes to be sold to civil airlines throughout the world. London-based companies like Vickers at Weybridge and DeHavilland at Colindale and Hatfield, were to benefit enormously from this government money for design and research. And in the early 1950s they seemed to be providing good value for money. The Vickers 'Viscount', equipped with jet turbo-prop engines, which ensured quiet and economical flights, quickly became the most successful British airliner ever made. There were large sales abroad, many of them to Commonwealth countries. And DeHavilland won the race to produce the world's first jet airliner when the Comet successfully came through its test flights in 1949 and 1950. Export orders to Commonwealth operators like Canadian Pacific Airlines and South African Airways, were to be one of the prizes of new developments like this.

However, the single most important export produced in London in the 1950s was motor vehicles. Much of this output came as

we shall see later – from the American-owned multinational of Fords at Dagenham, but there were also less prominent companies which boomed at this time. The most important of these were builders of buses and trucks.

Best known of all was the Associated Equipment Company chassis works at Southall, and its trading partner, the Park Royal BodyBuilders. Together they formed one of the biggest bus and truck manufacturers in Britain. For several decades they had established a reputation as the builders of London's buses. They had gradually been establishing an export business since the 1920s, but in the 1950s they began to export buses in earnest, particularly to the Commonwealth countries. Many major Commonwealth cities like Johannesburg and Pretoria in South Africa, and Melbourne and Adelaide in Australia, had large fleets of buses built in London, many of them strangely similar in appearance and design to the traditional double-decker London bus. Even far flung cor-

Above left: AEC workers pictured in the Southall factory in 1951. Every bus was tailor-made to customers' specifications

Top: AEC exported look-alike London buses all over the world, especially to the Commonwealth. It provided many fleets for South African cities like Johannesburg

Below: A blue and white liveried AEC bus pictured in Kuala Lumpur, Malaya (now Malaysia) in the early 1950s

ners of the Empire like Kuala Lumpur in Malaya had a fleet of blue and white liveried buses manufactured by AEC and Park Royal. To workers at AEC like Jack Ailsby, London was still the workshop of the world:

> It was a wonderful place to work in, we had a damn good team spirit; we were cock-a-hoop because we were the world leaders in producing trucks and buses. We had a fine body of craftsmen who produced these vehicles and they went all over the old Commonwealth and Empire, and the rest of the world as well. We were world renowned as the builders of London's buses and we felt we were world beaters. The original logo of AEC was a triangle and across the bottom was the word 'Southall', which was the base of the plant; wherever an AEC vehicle was exported so the name of Southall was exported with it, and it became synonymous with AEC. There was a great pride to think that the name Southall was on buses all over the world.

But if home-grown engineering firms were strengthening London's position as the workshop of the world, a new kind of company, the huge multinational, often American-owned, was growing in size and importance. Many of these giants had settled in the capital during the inter-war years and had been particularly attracted to cheap green-field sites in West London. More than half of these seventy or so major US companies could be found on the Great West Road, the North Circular Road and the Slough Trading Estate. It was around here that go-ahead American multinationals, like Hoover, Firestone Tyres and Gillette, built their art deco-style factories – monuments to the modern movement in architecture and to American enterprise in London. They had been drawn to the capital because it gave them access to a rich market at the heart of the Empire, and to protected Commonwealth and Empire markets.

Many of the multinationals boomed in the 1950s. In particular, Fords of Dagenham flourished. For after the war the world was hungry for cars and, with the European motor industry ravaged by the war, British-based companies like Fords had a virtual monopoly of exports. One of its most successful models at this time was the Zephyr, selling at £607. With the Consul and the Zodiac, it was one of a trio of scaled down American-style 'big cars', which became known as 'the Three Graces'. In the 1950s Fords were producing around a quarter of a million vehicles each year at Dagenham, most of which were exported. The output was phenomenal. To keep up with it they spent several millions of pounds

Ford assembly-line workers making Zephyrs at Dagenham. The workers were cogs in a giant machine, each one repeating the same minute task over and over again as the cars came down the line

on a brand new foundry which started operating in 1957.

Working for a multinational like Fords was very different to working in most of the smaller British companies, like AEC, which made great use of craft skills. To achieve the highest output for the lowest costs, mass assembly-line methods were used. At Fords the car frames moved slowly forward on a moving chain, known as the track. Workers were spread out along it and fitted engines, gearboxes, wheels and so on as the frames passed by. In order for the system to work smoothly, a rigid discipline was enforced by foremen. And there was an increasingly narrow division of labour, so that each worker performed just one kind of task which might take, say, two minutes to complete. Practically every year the company would try to increase productivity by reducing the time taken for each job at Dagenham. This was known to the workers as the 'speed-up', and it lay behind many disputes between men and management, as Bernie Passingham remembers:

> Working on the line was filthy, dirty and noisy. Basically, you had to have a bath every night. The metal dust that was flying around would turn all your underclothes rusty. No matter how much you washed the sheets they would go rusty and so would the pillows. But what really caused the trouble was the speed-up. We used to have a works standards man come round, and he'd time you with his watch. Then the foreman would come and say, 'Well, you've got to produce faster.' But it just didn't work out like that, because you felt you were working and sweating hard enough as it was. You were given so many seconds to do this and so many seconds to do that, and it didn't go down well with the workers. They were constantly cracking the whip and trying to get more and more out of us. Well, that annual time study caused lots of disputes and strikes. Sometimes the men would try to cheat the time-and-motion man by taking longer than they needed for the job while he was timing them, but they usually took that into account.

During the 1950s many companies in London compensated for increasingly monotonous work by using some of their profits to improve conditions for their workers. This was the heyday of company paternalism, when every major company felt it was essential to provide canteens, sports grounds, entertainments and paid holidays for workers. The aim was to generate a strong sense of community and loyalty revolving around the company. After the war Tate & Lyle helped to run a social club which organized Saturday night entertainment for its workers and their families and friends. Ron Linford recalls:

> It was known as the Tate & Lyle Saturday night out. It was really great. All the family would go including the kids. First thing we used to do was to make sure we had our seats right alongside the bar, so that we didn't have too far to carry the drinks. There was cabaret, fancy dress with prizes for the children, dancing to the band, spot waltzes and comedians doing turns. Sometimes they used to let all the balloons down at once. There used to be hundreds of them, and all the kids would dive towards them.

The 50s saw the heyday of company paternalism when many entertainments were provided for workers and their families. These photographs show (below) a cabaret act, (right) 'spot waltzes' and (bottom) balloons and party games for children – all regular features of Tate & Lyle Saturday night entertainment at the time

At AEC there was a huge range of social activities for the workforce. Jack Ailsby was involved in many of them:

> I was Chairman of the Sports Committee and we had clubs for everything: swimming, angling, football, rugby, cricket – the lot. I helped plan the annual gala day. I usually ended up running the coconut stall – that was a great laugh. Then we had all sorts of other things, like Christmas parties for the children and a club with cheap booze – you'd find me in there quite a lot! There was a feeling that the company was just one great big family.

But the great reward of increasing production and booming exports in London was fat pay packets. By the end of the 1950s the real income of working Londoners was almost double what it had been before the war. Until the mid-1950s rationing and consumer controls meant that there was no outlet for this increased spending power in the capital. But as soon as these were lifted Londoners began to enjoy the fruits of a new consumer society, based on mass-production. Labour-saving electric devices for the home, like washing-machines, refrigerators and vacuum cleaners, had previously been too expensive for most people outside the middle classes. But by the mid-1950s many Londoners could afford these 'luxury' items for the first time, even if they had to buy them on the 'never never', using hire purchase agreements. And it was now that most Londoners bought or rented their first television set. Jack Ailsby remembers:

> Everyone in the street had a television before us. I wasn't very interested because I was out all the time involved in the social

Television sets, record players and radios on display in a London electrical shop. Most Londoners' standard of living improved dramatically during the 50s as the capital enjoyed the fruits of a new consumer society

club and the union. The wife got a bit lonely and she wanted a television, but I didn't. Anyway, every evening I expected a hot dinner on the table when I came home, and I got one as well! But one day the wife went off and got some TV rental forms and when she served up the dinner she slapped them down on the table for me. She said, 'Right! We have a telly or you don't have any more hot dinners!' That was how we came to get our first television set.

By the late 1950s most Londoners would have agreed with Prime Minister Harold Macmillan that they had never had it so good. Many were enjoying a standard of living far above anything they had known before. But this industrial prosperity, at least as far as manufacturing industry was concerned, was largely based on the shaky foundations of London's dominant position in Commonwealth trade. This economic weakness was to be cruelly exposed in the next decade.

For during the 1960s the demand for independence in Britain's Empire and Commonwealth loosened or ended many of the old trading ties which had made London so rich: a stampede of twenty-seven colonies, most of them in Africa, the West Indies and the Mediterranean, became independent nations. The role call of colonies lost in the 1960s includes names like Cyprus (which was granted independence in 1960), Nigeria (1960), Jamaica (1962), Kenya (1963), Malta (1964), and Aden (1967). Added to this, South Africa severed her links with the Commonwealth in 1961.

These new nations, together with the old jewel in the crown India (which had achieved independence slightly earlier in 1947), could now choose their trading partners for the first time. And, overwhelmingly, they chose to turn away from the old dependency on London, developing their own industries and their own trading preferences. For Britain in the 1960s was being overshadowed by new industrial giants like America, the Soviet Union, Germany and Japan. They offered a big export market for the primary products of Commonwealth countries, and in return offered a wide range of manufactured goods that were often cheaper and more efficient than those made in Britain. Commonwealth countries flocked to trade in these new markets and exported to them direct, thus undermining London's entrepôt trade.

The result was that during the 1960s London's trade with the Commonwealth was halved. The old inner docks were the first to suffer. They were geared to the Commonwealth trade, situated as they were close to the commodity exchanges and all the elaborate warehousing and marketing services they involved. They also supplied many of the riverside factories which processed imported foods and raw materials from the Commonwealth. In 1967, due to falling trade, the East India Dock was closed, quickly followed by St Katherine's Docks and the London Docks in 1968. As a result, dock employment began to shrink. The number of lightermen fell dramatically, and a once thriving trade, handed down from father to son since the days of Empire, rapidly became almost extinct. Ken Rigby:

> The docks weren't doing so much business so in 1968 I thought I'd try something different and I moved out of lightering. A year later the lighterage company I worked for went out of business. My family had quite a few lightermen in it going back many years. My father had been one, and he used to take me out on the boats from the age of six. I'd taken the wheel of a barge when I was eight. I thought, to begin with, that one of my sons would follow me in the trade, but as the docks started to close there were just no opportunities; it was all dying out.

London's sugar industry was hit hard by independence and the break-up of the old Commonwealth trading links. New nations like India and Malaysia developed their own sugar refineries, and other governments (for example, in the West Indies), demanded greater control over their sugar crop and more money for what they produced. The consequence of all this was that Tate & Lyle's exports were halved and in 1967 they were forced to close down their refining operations at Plaistow Wharf. Ron Linford was one of the several hundred refinery workers who lost their jobs:

> When I took my severance pay and became unemployed I thought to myself, 'Well, I'll probably get a job somewhere else easy enough,' and at first I thought I'd have a few days off – it was a sort of novelty. Then I had to go and sign on. I'd never been to a Labour Exchange in my life, and it was horrible lining up there – I felt ashamed that you had to get in a queue and sign on, especially when you have worked all your life. Then I went to the Job Centre and the first words out of their mouths were 'How old are you?' 'I'm 47.' 'Sorry, you're too old, you stand no chance.' This was from a job centre! That was depressing in its own right, without having to go back and sit down and think to yourself: where can I go to look for a job? When can I go? I used to see adverts in papers, and went out after a few jobs, but when

I told them my age they'd say: 'Well, sorry, we're looking for somebody younger.' Day after day it was the same. I stayed at home and got very down. I regularly did two crosswords in the morning, then got some jobs done around the house.

Unemployment, which had been unknown in London throughout the 1950s, began to creep back into the capital in the 1960s, as many refineries, flour mills and factories in the docklands were forced to make cuts.

Job losses and company closures were made worse by the flood of cheap imports that were beginning to enter London from former Commonwealth countries. This was the real sting in the tail of the Empire. Worst affected was the capital's clothing industry. For more than a century many thousands of London's poor had toiled over sewing-machines in sweat shops, most of them in the East End and inner London, making shirts, coats and jackets for the metropolitan market. Traditionally, the hours had been long and wages low. But now these sweat shops and small factories were undercut by clothing made in places like India, Hong Kong and Taiwan, where the cost of labour was even cheaper than it was in London. An industry which after the war had employed around 150,000 was to be pruned to one-third of its original size.

London's newer industries – engineering, for example, concentrated in West London – were also beginning to shed workers. They too were undermined by the loss of the Commonwealth and tougher world competition. For many years there had been an emphasis on producing for 'soft markets': for example, exporting to less-developed countries or producing for government departments like the Ministry of Defence, which were playing an increasingly important role in the economy. These protected markets masked a growing inefficiency and lack of invention, and, when the crutch of Commonwealth based power and wealth was removed, the ailing nature of many companies was revealed. The answer in the 1960s seemed to be for competing companies to merge to form big corporations that would be more competitive on the world market. A fundamental change in the structure of London's newer industries was to result from this equation of size with efficiency.

What happened in London's aircraft industry was typical of this process. During the 1950s there had been more than a dozen separate plane-makers in the capital, each with their own highly paid design and construction teams oiled by government funds. The seeds of their decline were sown at this time when a number of projects went expensively and disastrously wrong. The most spectacular failure was the Comet, which after its early triumphs was involved in a series of tragic crashes caused by technical failures. As a result, it was grounded and withdrawn from service for several years. The government – which provided most of the important orders for both civil and military aircraft – insisted that the industry be streamlined in order to increase efficiency. The upshot of all this was that many famous names like Vickers and De-Havilland disappeared in the early 1960s, as most of London's plane-making companies were swallowed up into two giant corporations, Hawker Siddeley Aviation and the British Aircraft Corporation.

The new wave of corporatism was also felt in London's bus industry. In 1962 AEC and Park Royal were taken over by Leyland, and they in turn became part of the gigantic British Leyland Group when Leyland took over Austin and Morris in 1968. It was an attempt to combat increasing competition, especially in world markets where German and Japanese companies were beginning to win orders once held by Britain for buses and heavy vehicles. To begin with, the corporate power of the Lancashire-based Leyland company seemed to benefit the London end of the operation. In 1964, for example, the AEC division achieved record exports. However, in the long run the creation of this new breed of bigger company or corporation was to have a crippling effect on London's economy.

For many home-grown enterprises were being swallowed up into empires controlled by companies which had no commitment or loyalty to London. And, on a more modest level, small family firms were amalgamating into medium-sized companies which needed new sites. Increasingly, these bigger companies were coming to the conclusion that there was little reason to remain in the capital. Many firms operated in cramped sites and could not get planning permission to extend their premises, due to a long-standing post-war government policy to decentralize industry from London to avoid further congestion in the capital. Also London was an expensive place to be; rents and rates were spiralling, workers expected higher wages, and traffic congestion meant that transporting goods was difficult and costly. Thus it made sense for manufacturing concerns to move away from the capital. Many moved to new towns like Stevenage in Hertfordshire and Crawley in Surrey, or to green-field sites in the South East, where costs were much cheaper. The full impact of the exodus that was beginning would be felt in the next decade when the recession began to bite deep

The increasing size of companies through mergers and takeovers was, in a sense, an attempt to emulate the strength of huge American multinationals, like Fords, who were becoming more and more powerful during the 1960s. They had not been hit very hard by the decline of Commonwealth markets, because most of them were by now geared to sales in Britain and Europe. These giants were well equipped to prosper in an increasingly cutthroat and competitive world market, in which expensive machinery for mass production had to be constantly replaced and updated, and each company might need to spend millions of pounds each year on advertising alone.

Fords' great success story of the 1960s was the Cortina. Every part of the original version of this car was manufactured and assembled in the Dagenham plant, employing a work force that had increased to 30,000 by 1969. More than 4 million Cortinas were to run off the production-line at Dagenham, many of them for export. The millionth Cortina to be exported was transported by helicopter from Dagenham to Belgium amid much pomp and ceremony.

Despite the underlying weakness of London's economy, wages rose steadily for industrial workers in the 1960s. This new affluence meant that many working-class families were able to afford their first motor car. The 1960s were the decade of the so-called 'affluent worker', when it seemed inequalities of class were breaking down. The convoys of bicycles, which had once been a common sight entering factory gates all over London, were replaced by a convoy of cars edging their way into new factory car parks. Bernie Passingham was one of London's many industrial workers who bought a car for the first time in the early 1960s:

> Even though my job was making cars I never thought I'd own one – they were for the better off. But the wages improved a bit and the company had a sort of 'HP' scheme and you could buy second-hand cars with it. So I saved up for a long time and bought a Classic, and when I'd got it it was a big event. I'd built a garage years in advance but I couldn't actually drive a car. Now all I could afford was five lessons and, miraculously, I managed to pass my test after having just those five lessons. In the early days I was so proud of the car that I didn't want to get it dirty driving to work. So I used to leave it in the garage all day and go to work on the bike. We used the car at weekends and for holidays, and we had some lovely times.

The image of economic strength and vitality created by lots of donkey-jacketed workers driving expensive-looking cars around the capital was, however, an illusion. For, beneath this veneer of affluence, London's economy was in serious decline. In the 1970s and 80s its structural weaknesses which had begun to emerge in the previous decade were to be cruelly exposed. The result was to be the economic devastation of London's docklands and manufacturing industry, culminating in mass unemployment on a scale never before seen in the capital.

The pace of London's industrial decline quickened when Britain entered the EEC in early 1973. It was an attempt to sustain Britain's flagging economy through closer trading links with Europe at the expense of those with the Commonwealth. In place of the Commonwealth Preference System came high tariffs on Commonwealth imports and a quota on the amount of goods that could come in from outside Europe. These new restrictions, called the Common Agricultural Policy (CAP), hit the import of Commonwealth sugar, grain, and other foodstuffs very hard. And, predictably, London's old riverside economy of refineries, flour mills and food factories was undermined.

Tate & Lyle and London's sugar industry suffered seriously from EEC quotas on the import of sugar-cane. These quotas were designed to boost Europe's sugar-beet industry, which provided an alternative source of sugar. Sugar-beet refineries were not heavily dependent on imports and were located away from London, close to the point of production, like, for example, the huge sugar farms of East Anglia. As a result, Tate & Lyle's production was decimated in the 1970s, refineries at Fulham and Hammersmith were closed, and several thousand workers were made redundant.

The London docks themselves were also to be hit. Entry into Europe reinforced changes in shipping routes which had for decades been taking trade away from London to booming continental ports like Rotterdam, Hamburg and Dunkirk. Whereas the Port of London had merely been patched up after the war, these ports had enjoyed massive investment and now offered superior dock and warehouse facilities. Also, the shift away from deep-sea Commonwealth trade to short-sea European trade, which came with Britain's entry into the EEC, greatly favoured coastal ports close to the continent at London's expense. Channel ports like Dover and Felixstowe were better placed and better equipped to deal with the growing trade with Europe than the London dock system, which was geared to the old-style trade with the Commonwealth and Empire. In the eyes of employers, these ports enjoyed the further advantage of not being tied up by trade-union agreements, which they believed had caused overmanning and strikes in the London docks. Sadly, the London dockers' militant struggle for

Above: Derelict warehouses and barges on the riverside. From the late 60s onwards the inner London docks went into rapid decline. St Katherine's Docks (right) emerged in the 1970s to become a popular tourist attraction. Here we see, from left to right: the Tower Hotel, the yachting marina and the old tea warehouse

better job security and wages, culminating in the end of the casual dock labour system, coincided with the rapid decline in the port's trade and importance.

To survive, the Port of London Authority cut its labour costs dramatically by investing all its resources in containerization at Tilbury, Essex, which had the advantage of deep-water facilities and was closer to the Continent. From now on, most goods would be loaded and unloaded in huge containers. One by one all the old inner docks were closed down, ending with the Royals in 1981. Such closures were attractive to the PLA and promised big profits because they released many acres of dockland that were ripe for development as hotels, luxury apartments and offices. It was the end of an era for a labour force of around 20,000 people who had once made the docks rich. Ironically, the dockers' battle for job security had ended with many having no job at all.

To make matters worse, the dock closure had a knock-on effect which further damaged traditional employment in the docklands. For every job lost in the docks, another three were lost in dock-related services and industries. Ship-building and transport companies went to the wall. And more and more of the riverside factories either closed down or moved away from Central London, as sea-borne supplies of raw materials, upon which they depended for survival, became difficult or impossible to obtain. The main artery of the system of world trade built up over 150 years of imperial history was now severed. Unemployment in the dockland boroughs of Tower Hamlets, Newham and Southwark increased from 10,000 in the late 1960s to 80,000 by the early 80s.

The decline of London's manufacturing industry was accelerated even more by the oil crisis and the world economic recession which followed in its wake from 1973 onwards. Its economy was too weak to adapt to the spiralling costs of fuel and the loss of markets that it now faced. As a result, the blight of company closures and rising unemployment spread out from the docklands to engulf the whole of the capital. Employment in manufacturing industry was to be almost halved, falling from a million in 1973 to just over half a million ten years later. The area hit hardest was the once prosperous industrial belt of West London. For it was in the engineering and electrical industries, concentrated in outer boroughs like Ealing and Hounslow, that most of the damage was inflicted. These industries lost a staggering 150,000 jobs in Greater London in the ten years after 1973. During this time Ealing was losing jobs at the rate of over 2000 each year.

One major cause of this decline was the decision of a number of big companies and corporations to leave London. The exodus had begun in the 1960s, but it was in the 70s that its full impact was felt. The recession forced companies to rationalize their operations in order to survive. And one easy way for them to save money was to reduce or completely close down their factories in the capital. Rents and rates were rising fast, and traffic congestion and labour relations were getting worse. On top of this, there were two positive incentives to move elsewhere. Generous government grants were available for companies setting up in the region. And the property boom in the capital meant that companies could 'asset-strip' their factory sites, and make an enormous amount of money out of redeveloping them for offices and warehouses.

Underlying the decision of many companies to leave London was the fact that they had outgrown any roots in the capital and had little commitment to it or its workers. What resulted was a stampede of engineering and electrical industries out of London from the early 1970s onwards leaving countless casualties in its wake. British Aerospace shed 2000 jobs from Kingston-upon-Thames; Westland shed 2000 jobs in helicopter production from Hayes as they moved their operations to Yeovil in Somerset; the General Electric Company shed 6000 jobs from their factories making electrical products in Willesden; Lucas shed 1500 jobs in auto-products from Acton; Delta Rolling Mills shed 1000 engineering jobs in Ealing; and Thorn-EMI shed 2000 jobs in their factories making electrical products in Hayes and Ilford. A number of companies were establishing new plants in the Western Corridor, extending fifteen miles either side of the M4, out as far as Bristol. This was to become known as 'the Sunrise Belt'; here companies could enjoy better communications and a better environment than in the capital.

One of the saddest casualties of this race to get out of London was the home-grown bus and heavy truck industry. For between 1979 and 1981 British Leyland closed down AEC and Park Royal, with a loss of 3500 jobs. It was ironic that the death of these two companies, once proud suppliers of buses to London and its Commonwealth and Empire, meant that now no more buses would be made in the capital at all.

The closure – like other major industrial closures in London – dealt a cruel blow to the local community which depended on the factory. AEC in Southall had once employed 4000 men and women, making it the most important source of work in the area. Many of the employees who remained had spent all or most of their working lives with the company. One of them was Jack Ailsby:

> When the company closed it was a devastating blow. It had been my life, twenty-four hours a day. I was always doing something there, either working or drinking in the bar or helping on the sports committee. The day it closed down a lot of people cried and some of my friends had nervous breakdowns over it. The company had been so important to the local community, and now all that just went.

As British-owned manufacturing corporations moved out or closed down their London operations, American multinationals, like Fords, Hoover and Kodak, became one of the last strongholds of secure industrial work in and around the capital. However, the world recession was also to lead them to move work out of London. The art deco-style factories on the Great West Road and Western Avenue quickly became museum pieces, as the departure of multinationals turned a great swathe of West London into an industrial wilderness. Hoover stopped manufacturing at Perivale with a loss of 11,000 jobs, and Firestone Tyres and Trico-Folberth wound down their operations adding another 2500 job losses. The great Hoover factory remains, but only as an elegant frontage for the company's office headquarters, testimony to the changing economy in the area which has become dominated by offices and warehouses. Companies like these left for all the same kinds of reasons that had lured British companies away in their search to cut costs and maintain profits.

However, the American multinationals were often not moving to other parts of Britain, but to other parts of the world. In the wake of the world recession many foreign countries were competing fiercely for their custom in order to boost their sagging economies. Multinationals thus began following government grants and cheap labour all over the world. Electrical and engineering com-

Inset: Jack Ailsby in his last days at AEC. The company, with its trading partner Park Royal Body Builders, was closed down between 1979 and 1981 with a loss of 3500 jobs

Left: Ford workers occupying the Dagenham plant in a battle with management over layoff compensation during the late 70s

panies tended to move to the continent – their principal market. This was to have two main effects on London's economy. Firstly, it meant a reduction in jobs. Secondly, it meant that factories that remained in the capital were drawn increasingly into an international division of labour.

Fords of Dagenham provide the classic case study of this kind of development. Since the war Fords were London's biggest manufacturing employer, but in the five years after 1979 they shed 10,000 out of 30,000 jobs they provided in the capital. This resulted from Fords' policy of redirecting work to other plants across the world. In 1975, for example, they established a major new factory in Valencia, Spain. By 1979 half the Fiesta cars sold in Britain would be made there. Also, as the Dagenham plant was drawn more and more into Fords' international division of labour, the work done there changed. Whereas in the old days cars like the Zephyr and the Cortina were completely made at Dagenham, now much of the work involved assembling parts imported from overseas. This trend, which meant the Dagenham factory was turning into an assembly plant, employing fewer skilled workers, was given a further impetus by the closure of its foundry in 1984. Most of Fords' job losses were accounted for by voluntary redundancies. Many older workers, like Bernie Passingham, were keen to accept a golden handshake because they felt angry and disillusioned about Dagenham's decline:

> Lots took early retirement like myself because the truth was they just didn't like working there, and it was a good excuse to get

> out. I felt sad because I felt we'd done a lot for the Ford Motor Company as workers. We worked hard, they made good profits – damned good profits – and they'd been used to buy and build plants abroad and not in the UK. That was sad because we were slowly losing out and becoming a screwdriver plant. To me that is morally wrong.

This multinational withdrawal from the capital had by the mid-1980s accounted, either directly or indirectly, for the loss of around 100,000 jobs in ten years. With altogether a million unemployed in London, its economy had become precariously dependent on them. For, by this time, multinational companies – most of them British or American – dominated London's manufacturing economy. They provided around 150,000 out of the half million industrial jobs remaining in the capital. Of the 75 manufacturing companies employing more than 500 workers in London, 72 were multinationals. And, because these giants occupied the commanding heights of London's economy, around another 150,000 jobs were tied up in smaller companies which serviced their needs for components and machinery. The dependency of London on these giants was the culmination of two and a half decades of decline following the break-up of London's Commonwealth and Empire trading links.

The final irony in the tale of London's international decline as a centre of trade and industry has been the boom in international tourism which has paralleled it. As factories moved out, so droves of foreign tourists moved into the capital. The take-off began in the 1960s, and ten years later tourism had become London's fastest growing industry. London, once the workshop of the world, was rapidly becoming the world's playground.

There was a clear link between industrial decline and the growth of tourism in London. For what lay behind the tourist boom was the fact that many more nations now had the industrial wealth to finance mass tourism to places like London. And they arrived at Heathrow airport in their millions in the new era of the charter flight. By the mid-1980s London attracted every year two million visitors from the United States, a grand total of one million from the former Commonwealth countries of Canada, Australia, South Africa and New Zealand, more than half a million from both West Germany and France, and another half a million from the Middle East. The London Tourist Board calculated that these overseas visitors spent a total of £2.5 billion each year in the capital, which worked out at £369 for each foreign tourist.

Visitors come to London because of its history. Featuring high in

London's top ten tourist attractions are its museums; number one in recent years has been the British Museum, where visitors can view an array of art treasures, most of them assembled during the great days of Empire and Commonwealth.

Many of the visitors from overseas are housed in luxury high-rise hotels in the West End, built during the late 1960s and early 70s. The tourists use the West End as a base to enjoy a hectic social round of sightseeing, theatre-going and expensive eating and drinking. In some ways their presence echoes the old aristocratic season which, like the tourists season, peaked during the spring and summer. And just as the Victorian season demanded a mass of servants to keep everything going, so the new one demands an army of catering staff, chambermaids, shop assistants, taxi drivers and tourist guides to service their needs. Today one in ten jobs in London is connected to tourism.

Some of those who would have worked in the docks and manufacturing industries now work in tourism. But the jobs available are a far cry from those which were enjoyed in the 1950s, when many young men entering lightering and manufacturing industry in the capital served a five-year apprenticeship and learnt a skill. Most of the work in the tourist industry is semi-skilled or unskilled, poorly paid and casual – in a sense these jobs directly parallel those done by the London poor who serviced the rich in their social season in the nineteenth century. One of the few jobs in which lightermen, for example, could hope to use some of their old skills was in the pleasure cruise business. Ken Rigby has worked on Thames pleasure cruises since 1976. He was grateful to find a job working on the river but it is rather boring compared to his old work as a lighterman, 'like driving a bus up and down the river all day'.

The most popular up-and-coming new attraction in recent years has been St Katherine's docks. Just a hundred years ago they were a treasure store of ivory, silver and spices from all over the world. Today the dock basin has been developed to include a luxury hotel and an assortment of chi-chi tourist shops and eating places. It is a favourite with Commonwealth visitors from countries like Nigeria, India and Hong Kong. They can gaze at the collection of old ships that date back to the days of Empire when their economy was dependent on London's sea going trade. Those days are now gone forever. For the Empire trade has now in some ways turned full circle. Once London prospered off the backs of the colonies and world trade. Now, having little manufacturing industry and a million unemployed to support, she is happy to service the needs of tourists and make a living from their new wealth.

CHAPTER 2
Style Capital

In the spring of 1966 the influential American magazine *Time* devoted its front cover to a pop art representation of London. Amongst the familiar images of Big Ben and the London bus were new and exciting ones: a mouthing pop star wearing a T-shirt with The Who and a 'British-made' symbol emblazoned across it; a spindly long-haired girl wearing dark glasses and a short dress with strange black and white geometric patterns; and a discotheque. The headline read: 'LONDON – THE SWINGING CITY.' In the article that accompanied this unprecedented front-page cover, *Time*'s London-based correspondent wrote:

> in this century every decade has its city. During the shell-shocked 1940s thrusting New York led the way, and in the uneasy 50s it was the easy Rome of *La Dolce Vita*. Today it is London, a city steeped in tradition, seized by change, liberated by affluence, graced by daffodils and anemones, so green with parks and squares that, as the saying goes, you can walk across it on the grass. In a decade dominated by youth, London has burst into bloom. It swings, it is the scene.

By the mid-1960s London had become *the* major international centre for fashion, design and music. These were the boom industries of the decade. They, in turn, boosted a whole range of smaller industries, like photography, modelling, magazine publishing, advertising and so on, which also clustered in the capital. These industries not only created immense wealth and provided work – directly or indirectly – for almost a quarter of a million Londoners; they also gave London a new image and its people a new sense of identity and vitality. The old pride in London as the heart of the Empire was eclipsed by a 1960s-style patriotism – felt very strongly by the younger generation – based on the city's leading position in the popular arts. This chapter tells the story of how London became the style capital of the world.

Immediately after the Second World War there were few signs of the explosion of popular culture that was to emerge in the 'swinging 60s'. London was a grey city dominated by austerity. Everything was on ration from shoes to sweets, and from meat to petrol. Clothes had to be bought with coupons saved over many

Opposite: Carnaby Street, Soho, in the summer of 1967. This street, with its great array of trend-setting boutiques, came to epitomize 'Swinging London' which had reached its height of fame a year before. In the mid-60s young people from all over Britain and tourists from all over the world flocked to this street to buy the latest fashions

months; the more enterprising people would make their clothes from curtain material. Things were in such short supply that there was a flourishing black market in most items. On many street corners 'spivs' could be seen selling – at a price – that most coveted of all articles, nylon stockings. Those women who were unable to afford a pair on the black-market sometimes drew a simple black line up the back of each bare leg to make it look as if they were wearing nylons. This was the limit of style for them.

Style was essentially the preserve of the rich, as it had always been. And London took its influences from other European cities, mainly Paris with its *haute couture*. Even hairdressers had to adopt the style and mannerisms of the French if they wanted to be successful. Raymond, the son of an Italian immigrant born in Soho and later to be known as Mr Teasie-Weasie, took advantage of this fascination, with all things French in his high-class salons during the early 1950s.

> Women at that time thought that only good hairdressing could come from French hairdressers. So I taught my stylists to use French expressions, such as *'Bonjour, Madame,' 'Comment allez-vous, Madame?'* and all that nonsense. I also renamed

Mr Teasie-Weasie in one of his London salons in 1951 applies the finishing touches to a hair style for film star Googie Withers. At this time style was the preserve of the rich and was strongly influenced by Parisian *haute couture*

> them. If their name was Joe I called them Louis or Monsieur Emile. They were all given a new name, French sounding.

While the rich monopolized the world of fashion, the older generation imprinted itself on practically all the activities and entertainments available for young people. The immediate post-war years witnessed the zenith of traditional values, old pastimes and adult authority. Church attendance in the capital rose, as did membership of political parties and youth organizations like the Boy Scouts, and family life flourished. The main entertainments were watching football, going to the cinema, and rambling or cycling, and sometimes whole families would be involved in these activities. In the late 1940s attendances at football matches peaked: top London clubs like Arsenal and Tottenham often had gates of over 50,000. Going to matches was often a family affair and many fathers and sons would go together. The reason for this resurgence of the old established ways was the fact that Londoners had been deprived of these simple and familiar pastimes during the war; they now resumed them with renewed vigour. Also, one of the legacies of the war was an enthusiasm for communal activities. And, on top of this, lack of money meant that most people couldn't afford anything more grand.

Although this post-war culture was in retrospect rather cosy and high minded, it was at the time very restricting and regimented for young people. Fathers and elder brothers who spent several years in the forces returned home and reasserted the old discipline which had been loosened during the war. This discipline was reinforced in the classroom by school teachers and in the street by policemen who were now back to full strength. The sexual permissiveness and relaxation of moral standards which had been a feature of the war years also ended abruptly when family life resumed. Many London dance halls had rules which quite tightly controlled the dress and behaviour of their customers, and the more adventurous dances like the American jitterbug were banned in some places. John Kerridge who grew up in Wood Green, North London, in the early 1950s remembers the tedium of the weekly routine of visits to the cinema and to relatives:

> The pictures used to be packed every night, night after night, because there was practically nothing else to do. People used to wait out in the cold for ages waiting to get inside. All the time, you did as you were told. And you did a lot of visiting to relations. You'd go round to tea on a Sunday afternoon and have a family get-together. But you didn't have a choice. 'Sunday afternoon, you're coming with us to see gran', and that was it.

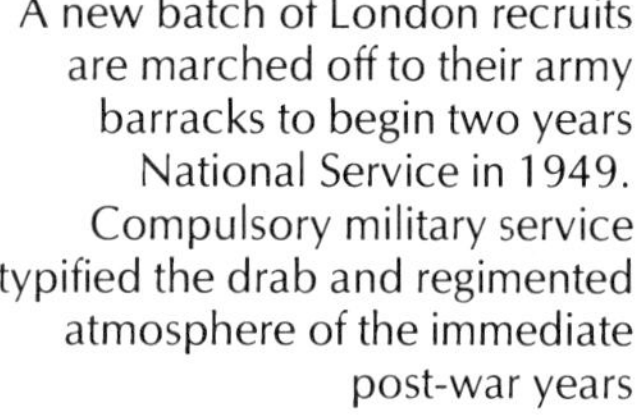

A new batch of London recruits are marched off to their army barracks to begin two years National Service in 1949. Compulsory military service typified the drab and regimented atmosphere of the immediate post-war years

Young men at this time were also confronted by the daunting prospect of National Service. Under the terms of the National Service Act of 1948 they were called up at the age of eighteen to undergo two years' military training and service. This was the first time that compulsory military service had been seen in Britain outside wartime. Most found the experience boring and oppressive.

The conformity, regimentation and intense drabness of the world that young people were growing into provided a great spur for them to revolt. And during the early 1950s they began to rebel against the stranglehold that the older generation and the rich exercised over style and entertainment. Bohemian sub-cultures, celebrating an unconventional kind of individualism, spontaneity and style, began to emerge in the capital.

Soho was the first and the most important centre of the capital's underground culture, paving the way for the area to become later the heart of Swinging London. It had established itself as an artistic Bohemia in the late 1930s, attracting literary figures like the poet, Dylan Thomas. After the war the bars and restaurants in Soho continued to attract Bohemians. But there was a shift in emphasis from literarure to music. Jazz became the driving force for this alternative culture, and by the early 1950s jazz basement clubs honeycombed the streets of Soho. One of the first was the Club 11, which opened in 1948 on the corner of Windmill Street and Archer Street, and was run by jazz musicians Ronnie Scott and John Dankworth. Marijuana smoking was very popular amongst jazz musicians at the time, and the club was raided by the police and later closed down as a result. Shortly afterwards the premises became Cy Laurie's Jazz Club, one of the major jazz venues in the country. It was here that in 1951 singer George Melly helped to organize one of London's first all-night jazz sessions – at the time a very daring and exciting idea.

While jazz clubs were becoming established in Soho, another meeting place for young people took off in the area – the coffee

Left: Jazz at a Soho nightclub in the mid-50s. Soho was the first centre of London's 'underground' youth culture, and jazz was the driving force behind it

Above: A young George Melly pictured in Soho in 1951. In this year he organized one of London's first all-night jazz sessions at Cy Laurie's jazz club

bar. Serving Italian-style espresso coffee, and providing a juke box and regular live music, including jazz or skiffle groups, these coffee bars, many of which stayed open virtually all night, acquired a powerful mystique as oases of alternative culture in London. The first to open in 1953 was the Mika in Frith Street, but as the coffee bars boomed it was surpassed by Heaven and Hell in Old Compton Street, and the Home of Sam Widges on the corner of Berwick Street.

By the mid-1950s these new trends were attracting national and even international interest; their followers were insultingly dubbed by the press 'bums,' 'beats', and 'beatniks'. The young people themselves, eager to acquire a different identity to that of 'square' society, adopted these names, and a new beatnik sub-culture was born.

Most of the beatniks were young and middle class, often aspiring actors, artists or students. Because there was such a concentration of them in London the heart of the beatnik culture remained in Soho. However, many beatniks looked to the Parisian Left Bank and the existential philosophy of Jean-Paul Sartre for inspiration. This reflected their rejection of narrow British values and their interest in exploring the individual psyche. The life style which emerged valued spontaneity and creativity above all else, and this, in turn, promoted a love for jazz improvisation, poetry and anything unconventional. There was also a sharp political edge to this subculture and it provided strong support for the first 'Ban the Bomb' Aldermaston marches and Trafalgar Square demonstrations of the early CND.

Young Bohemians expressed their group identity and their rebellion in the way they dressed. They chose casual and informal clothes, which to outsiders appeared very scruffy. Peter Powell, an aspiring actor in London during the early 1950s, remembers how he dressed:

> In the 50s everybody was very stereotyped and the clothes they wore were sports jackets, flannels and a collar and tie, and possibly suede shoes if you were really daring. I guess for the kind of people we were, who were beat, we wanted to look different. Big baggy sweaters were *de rigueur*. Probably the holier the better. Then you would have corduroy trousers, often tied with string or enormous belts, and cravats or scarves tied round your neck.

Although beatniks dressed informally most of the time, they also loved to wear outrageous unconventional gear, especially for jazz dancing. Amongst the devotees of this new Bohemian culture were many young people who were later to rise to fame in the London fashion world of the 1960s. For example, two former art students of Goldsmith's College, Mary Quant and her then boyfriend Alexander Plunket Green, were regulars at Humphrey Lyttleton's jazz club in Oxford Street. They were noted for their unique style of dress. Alexander Plunket Green:

> My mother had been ill for a long time and I had no money, and I actually wore all her clothes all the time. I didn't wear frocks exactly, but I put on pyjamas and trousers which had zips up the side and that sort of thing. But when I got a big bigger and couldn't get into her blouses anymore I used to paint buttons on my chest and just wear a tie with it, and pretend I had a shirt on.

Mary Quant:

> I hated the clothes the way they were so I used to make circular skirts out of marvellous great prints and find black tights from theatrical costumiers and black ballet shoes and black leotard tops, and these skirts were really great to dance in.

After Mary Quant left art college she worked in a high-class milliners. Her real ambition, however, lay in designing alternative styles of dress to those which she saw all around her in the London of the mid-1950s. Mary Quant:

> What I loathed was the unsexiness, the lack of gaity, the formal stuffiness of the look that was said to be fashion. I wanted

clothes that were much more for life – much more for real people, much more for being young and alive in.

After long discussions in the coffee bars and jazz clubs she decided to go it alone and in 1955 opened Bazaar, London's first boutique. Located in King's Road, Chelsea, the boutique's distinctive feature was its free and easy atmosphere, which allowed customers to browse around and try clothes on unattended, contrasting sharply with the formal ways of the old clothes shops. All the designs sold in Bazaar were by Quant. A further break with tradition came when Alexander Plunket Green opened a restaurant in the basement. Both enterprises were extremely successful.

It was around this time that King's Road began to take off as another centre of alternative culture for the young alongside Soho. By the mid-1950s coffee bars, soup kitchens, small clothes shops and jazz clubs were sprouting up all over Chelsea. These were prototype bistros, boutiques and night clubs, that were to become all the rage in Swinging London in several years' time. They were overwhelmingly peopled by the young middle classes, the more stylish of whom were dubbed by the press 'the Chelsea Set'. Few young Londoners from a working-class background felt at ease in them, and they became the preserve of people who had been to grammar school or had enjoyed higher education.

So London's working-class youth developed their own subcultural style, that of the Teddy Boy. The term was first coined in the early 1950s as a derogatory reference to South London teenagers who 'took over' the latest style for the rich. Savile Row was attempting to relaunch the 'look' of the Edwardian dandy for young aristocratic men about town. The Teddy Boys adopted the

Below left: Teddy Boys pictured in a night club in 1955. This male-dominated sub-culture originated in South London in the early 50s and was overwhelmingly working class in character

Below: Jiving in a London night club in the mid-50s

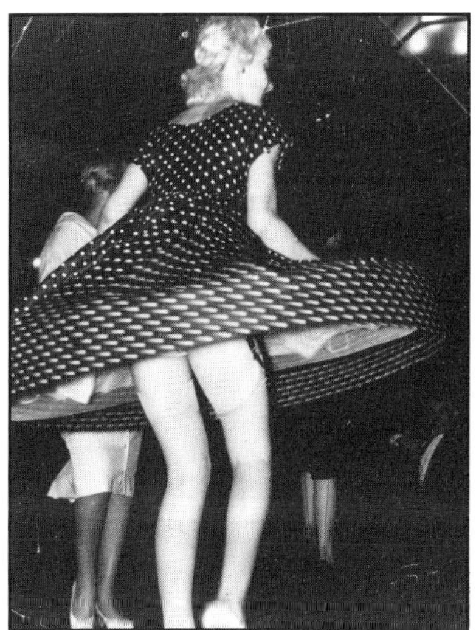

drape jackets and velvet collars from this fashion and combined them with drainpipe trousers or jeans and bootlace ties, which they had seen American cowboys wearing in films. This was to be the distinctive uniform of the 'Teds'.

Although in the press Teds were widely associated with gang violence, in fact their most treasured possession was not the flick knife but the comb. The tone of this new sub-culture was extremely narcissistic. Teddy Boy violence often arose as a result of their over-reacting to insults about their dress. For example, the first Teddy Boy murder on Clapham Common in 1953 occurred after a youth taunted a Ted with the words 'flash cunt'. A well-groomed quiff and Brylcreemed hair added the finishing touches to the slick image that Teds were cultivating. Traditional 'bob-a-knob' barbers whose repertoire was limited to short back and sides had to adapt quickly to the changing fashions. Brian Fleiss, an early Teddy boy in Burnt Oak, North London, remembers: 'You used to go in and ask for a Tony Curtis, and get the barber to put a quiff on the front. I'd tell him I wanted plenty on the front.'

Despite the fact that the Teddy Boy culture was – as its name suggests – male dominated, girls were also involved and influenced by it, and they too developed a distinctive style of dress. Jackie Fleiss recalls:

> We wore jeans a lot. They weren't tailored then – they were pretty baggy and never tight enough so we used to start off by getting in a bath full of water with the jeans on and shrink them to fit you. But it was very uncomfortable letting jeans dry on you and your parents didn't like that at all. And we used to have full skirts with thick petticoats underneath made of a material called Vylene. And you'd have maybe three or four of these things, which we used to starch. After you'd washed them and taken them off the line they were so stiff they'd stand up on their own. But they were terrific for jiving. And we always had black stockings and suspenders. You didn't have tights in those days, only nylons.

Once again, the driving force behind this new sub-culture was music. But while the beatniks raved about jazz, the Teddy Boys were devoted followers of the Rock 'n' Roll music that was arriving from America. It featured the electric guitar and was loud, brash and aggressive. To the older generation this new music seemed discordant and disturbing. But the explosive sounds of Bill Haley and Elvis Presley captured the mood of the younger generation and their yearning for greater freedom. Brian Fleiss:

I remember hearing Bill Haley and the Comets' 'Rock Around

> the Clock' in 1956, and I thought to myself, I haven't heard anything like this before – this is really wild stuff. It was just something that I had to be involved in. There was nothing before that, you were in the family environment. But through this teenagers began to break out on their own; you could identify with it.

The most important institution for London Teds was the Saturday night 'hop' at the local dance hall. Here their two passions for music and dress could be indulged. The ability to jive impressively was of paramount importance and many weeks would be spent learning the latest steps and movements. John Kerridge remembers:

> If you didn't have a partner you'd go up to the bedroom with the Dansette, put the records on and use the door handle. And there you'd be shaking and turning around and using the door handle as though it were your partner.

Teddy Boy culture never really penetrated the more Bohemian central areas like Soho and Chelsea and became very much a phenomenon of working-class districts like Clapham and Stepney. However, one Soho coffee bar did become popular with Teds and developed into a famous breeding-ground for British Rock 'n' Roll performers. This was the 2 i's in Old Compton Street: it was here that Tommy Hicks, Harry Webb and Terry Nelhams began their careers. They later changed their names to Tommy Steele, Cliff Richard and Adam Faith.

The 2 i's coffee bar in Old Compton Street, Soho, in the late 50s. It was here that rock and roll stars like Tommy Steele, Cliff Richard and Adam Faith were 'discovered'

The Teddy Boys and the Beatniks then were pioneers, breaking new ground and flouting the old conventions. They created new and exciting dress and music fashions for young people in a grey, conformist world. However, by 1958 both movements had become rather stale and predictable and London's youth was searching for something different. What they came up with was the Mod cult. The styles they generated were the real powerhouse behind the Swinging London explosion of the mid-1960s. Whereas the Teddy Boys and Beatniks had only involved and influenced a minority of young people, the Mod style became a mass phenomenon.

Mods were much more smooth and sophisticated than were Teddy Boys or Beatniks. It all started in 1958 when a small group of male youths, some of them sons of tailors living in Stepney and Stamford Hill, adopted a new look which was a combination of Italian and French styles. Impeccably cut Italian suits with very narrow lapels were tailor-made for them, and worn with hand-made winkle picker shoes and shirts with pointed collars. The image was completed by a short, neat Italian or French hair style, copied from foreign film stars of the day like Alain Delon – very different to the greasy, Brylcreemed look of the Teddy boy. One of the pioneers of the new look, Islington born Willy Deacey, then an apprentice printer, remembers taking great trouble to get the hair right:

> Most of us had terrific hair, French style, and you spent a lot of time on it. You had to use sugar water. What you would do was wash your hair, then get a bowl of hot water, put sugar in it, then let it cool and keep stirring it up and then plaster that on your head to get it into shape. You used to leave it on all night – the longer you left it on the better it was. If you had straight hair you left it on twenty-four hours. It was horrible stuff. But if you had crinkly hair you might have to leave it on for four days. I knew one guy, a friend of mine called Gypo, he had to keep it on four days and he just put a sort of balaclava thing over his head, but it still didn't work. But with straight hair it came out just the business.

Mods spent most of their money on clothes and were obsessively fastidious about their appearance. Willy Deacey:

> We used to go to a lot of extremes. Once I didn't go out because I put on my suit, and my shoes were a little bit dirty so I got the polish out and – disaster – I looked in the mirror and I'd splat-

> tered my shirt. So I got the hump and I didn't go out that evening; I stayed in because my shirt wasn't perfect. And I knew guys who'd get on a bus with a sheet of brown paper so they could put it on the seat so they didn't get any dirt on their suit. And they'd sit bolt upright so they were not touching the seat. I used to go to the Tottenham Royal and I knew this guy who would turn up from a building site in his wellies and a pickaxe, and with a suitcase, and he went into a cloakroom and cleaned up and came out in a suit, tie, shirt, shoes, socks that he had in the case. Because he was working so far away he couldn't get home and he thought he'd do it there. We took it very seriously and you had to be immaculate, very dandyish.

One of their other main interests was the modern jazz music of people like Dave Brubeck and Charlie Mingus. Modern jazz provided a 'cool' sound which matched their image, and it was this avant-garde taste in music that inspired them to call themselves Modernists. True to their name, the Modernists loved everything that was modern and many dreamed of owning a car like an E-type Jag. However, because most of them were still apprentices or worked at a lowly level in London's factories and offices, they had to make do with motor scooters for getting around. The most popular ones were the Italia Lambrettas and Vespas which had a sleek shape and enjoyed the added advantage of being less oily than motor bikes. Soon the Modernists took to wearing parkas – all-weather cape-shaped coats – to protect their clothes and keep them clean and tidy. By 1960 the Modernists had become a minor cult in Soho's nightclubs. One favourite haunt was Le Kilt, which was frequented by young French women whose 'cool' image they greatly admired.

However, as late as 1960 the Mod cult had still not been discovered by the media, and it had only a few thousand teenage adherents scattered over London. Two key factors were to transform it into a mass commercial phenomenon and an internationally famous style. The first and most important was the constellation of changes associated with the development of a consumer society. Wages had been gradually improving since the war, but it was the period between 1958 and 1966 when the young really enjoyed the fruits of affluence. During this period the income of many young people almost doubled, and, according to some estimates, by the mid-1960s their earnings were four times greater than they had been thirty years before. Added to this, most working-class families were now so much better off there was a breakdown of the old tradition in which teenage sons and daughters had handed over most of their wages to their parents in order to help pay the family bills. This meant that, for the first time ever, young people were economically independent and had a substantial amount of disposable income. It was estimated in the early 1960s that the average weekly wage of teenagers was around £10; of this, about £7 was left as disposable income after they had paid for their 'keep' at home. Because wages were high in London, teenagers in the metropolis had more money at their disposal than young people anywhere else in Britain. Their spending power was increased by the rapid spread of hire purchase from the late 1950s onwards. And the economic importance of youth was heightened by the fact that in the early 1960s almost 40 per cent of the population were under twenty-five. The baby boom just after the war meant that Britain was increasingly becoming a young country. Youth suddenly became a very lucrative market to sell to and exploit.

Not only did young people have more money than ever before; they also had more free time. From the 1950s onwards the number of hours spent at work was gradually reduced; at the same time holidays with pay increased. Labour-saving innovations in the home, like washing-machines, vacuum cleaners and convenience foods, also created more free time, especially for girls who were no longer obliged to spend so much time tied to the home helping their mothers as they had in the past. And in 1960 National Service, which had deprived most teenage boys of two years of freedom, was abolished.

A new market catering for the needs and wants of young people was being opened up. The young were ripe for commercial exploitation and yet the large companies and corporations which dominated the world of fashion, design and music were staid and conservative in their approach. In the early 1960s the BBC, for example, were very reluctant to give any air time to pop music, either on radio or television. Many bosses were fearful that pandering to the whims of youth would unleash a dangerous, antisocial culture. This attitude was not unconnected to the fact that the teenage market was overwhelmingly working class in character and taste – many young people from middle-class backgrounds spent most of their teenage years in the education system and had little money to spend. There was an enormous amount of snobbery about catering for what were seen to be 'yobboish' tastes. As a result, the teenage market would be left wide open to young entrepreneurs who were very close to their customers in age and background, and knew what they wanted.

This was where the second key factor shaping the take-off of the

Mod cult came into play – education. Improvements in the education system following the 1944 Education Act meant that the quality of schooling and the opportunities available for working-class children were greater than they had ever been before. Although the system was still heavily biased against the working classes it did allow more young people from humble backgrounds to enter further and higher education. Before the war higher education had been largely the preserve of the middle and upper classes. However, the expansion of the higher education system in the post-war years and the development of a much broader and more generous system of grants meant that many more young people from working-class backgrounds could enjoy a college or university training. The new colleges and universities were to become a seed-bed for artists, designers, musicians and entrepreneurs of all sorts who catered for the teenage market. They were attracted by the excitement of an alternative career outside conventional society and had a natural feel for what teenagers wanted.

One of the main sources of young talent was art colleges. Before the war they had been little more than finishing schools for well-to-do young ladies who wished to learn genteel refinements like drawing and painting between leaving school and getting married. But by the early 1960s they had become much more dynamic places, encouraging students to question the status quo and teaching a whole range of commercial skills in graphics, design and fashion. And the new college life gave many more young people more time to think, develop and create their own personal style. There was a great concentration of art schools and colleges in the London area – Chelsea, St Martin's, Central, Camberwell, Kingston, Hornsey, Harrow, Wimbledon, Croydon, Sidcup and so on – and they were a magnet for young creative talent from over a wide area. Many leading figures in Swinging London – for example, musicians like Pete Townshend of The Who, Ray Davies of the Kinks and Keith Richard of the Rolling Stones – had been educated at art colleges in the capital.

Affluence and education were then the two main driving forces behind the explosion of the Mod cult into the Swinging London scene between 1958 and 1966. One created the big youth market and the other helped to create the young entrepreneurs to service and exploit it. The 'explosion' was a consequence of the close inter-action between the two groups.

The first sign that the Modernists cult was taking off was in the early 1960s when there was a rapid growth of boutiques selling clothes with a Mod look. These boutiques, like Mary Quant's prototype, were usually small, informal and friendly shops. They made shopping for clothes a lot easier and more enjoyable. And prices were usually fairly low. Often music would be blasted into the customer's ears from speakers fixed to the walls. In these shops budding Mods could spend their new wealth and indulge their tastes for smart and fashionable clothing to the full. Boutiques quickly spread all over London and there were about 1500 of them in the capital by the mid-1960s. They tended, however, to be concentrated in Carnaby Street in Soho and King's Road in Chelsea.

The boutiques in Carnaby Street were primarily for men. The male vanity of what was now called the Mod style meant that this represented a large share of the market. By the early 1960s half a dozen boutiques in this Soho back street were owned by one man, John Stephen, a Glaswegian grocer's son who came to London in 1956 when he was nineteen. He was the entrepreneur most in tune with the teenage Mod look which was both neat and flamboyant. He noticed what Mods were wearing and what they wanted, and the moment a new style appeared on the streets he began stocking it in his shops. Stephen revolutionized men's clothes. His first boutique, called His Clothes, was a mecca for top Mods. These fashion leaders were known in Mod circles as 'faces' and they would spend what were then astonishing sums of money on clothes. Some of the trendiest shirts would be sold for £4 or more which represented a huge chunk of their weekly wages. The 'faces' were excited by the huge displays of well-cut suits, jackets and trousers and the many different styles and fabrics available in Stephen's boutiques. All the latest Mod trends – like, for example, mohair suits or white suits – were anticipated and catered for by Stephen. And he also sold coloured hipster trousers which previously had been very hard to obtain and only homosexuals had dared to wear because of their supposedly effeminate colours. His shops played a major role in popularizing and commercializing Mod styles of dress for young men; they were sold first to a huge market in London and then all over Britain and the world. The rapid expansion of his chain of boutiques was quite remarkable. Within a few years he was a millionaire owning twenty-five boutiques in London, twenty-four in the United States and twenty-one in various European cities.

The boutiques which mushroomed in and around King's Road in Chelsea primarily catered for teenage girls and young women. They were run by an army of small entrepreneurs, many of them young art school graduates who made and marketed their own designs. The Mod look that they sold was often a refined version of what they had seen Mod girls wearing on the streets and in the club of London. Mod girls were always a minority in this male dominated sub-culture, but they too were obsessively concerned with their appearance and dress. The Mod fashion which was to make London world famous was, of course, the miniskirt, but this had been preceded by many equally adventurous fashions, for example, women wearing men's shirts and trousers. Some boutiques struggled to survive and a few went bust, but towering above all of them were a handful of giants, the most successful of which was Mary Quant's Bazaar. Her simple bright designs always stayed one step ahead of her competitors and she became the most fashionable purveyor and popularizer of the Mod look. By the early 1960s she and Alexander Plunket Green – who was now her husband and business partner – realized that the appeal of their clothes was no longer limited to their friends in Chelsea. Alexander Plunket Green:

> At first we thought it was just the art studenty type that wanted to look like us and buy our clothes. But what we didn't realize at the time and didn't discover for some time was the fact that we were interpreting the mood of the whole generation, not just smart art students. The whole thing caught on in a much bigger way than we'd expected. We thought we were just working for people who lived in Chelsea, but the whole thing was actually what people wanted from all over.

The Mod look for young women spread all over London by the early 1960s then all over Britain and the United States in the next three years. As Quant's confidence grew so did her attacks on the fashion establishment. She changed the whole concept of the fashion show, for example, which until then had been very staid and demure. The women who modelled her clothes were instructed to run, jump and dance down the catwalk, often with a group providing live backing music. Controversial exploits like these attracted even more publicity which in turn generated bigger export orders. By the mid-1960s there was an insatiable demand for Quant-designed clothes on licence all over the world. And in 1966 she received the OBE for her services to exports.

What really enabled the styles of London's leading designers like Quant to reach a mass audience was fashion journalism in newspapers and glossy magazines like *Nova, Queen* and the *Sunday Times* colour supplement, which began in 1962. A young generation of fashion journalists in the early 1960s eagerly embraced the Mod look. The awesome power of fashion pages to set trends was enhanced by the greater use of photographs, even

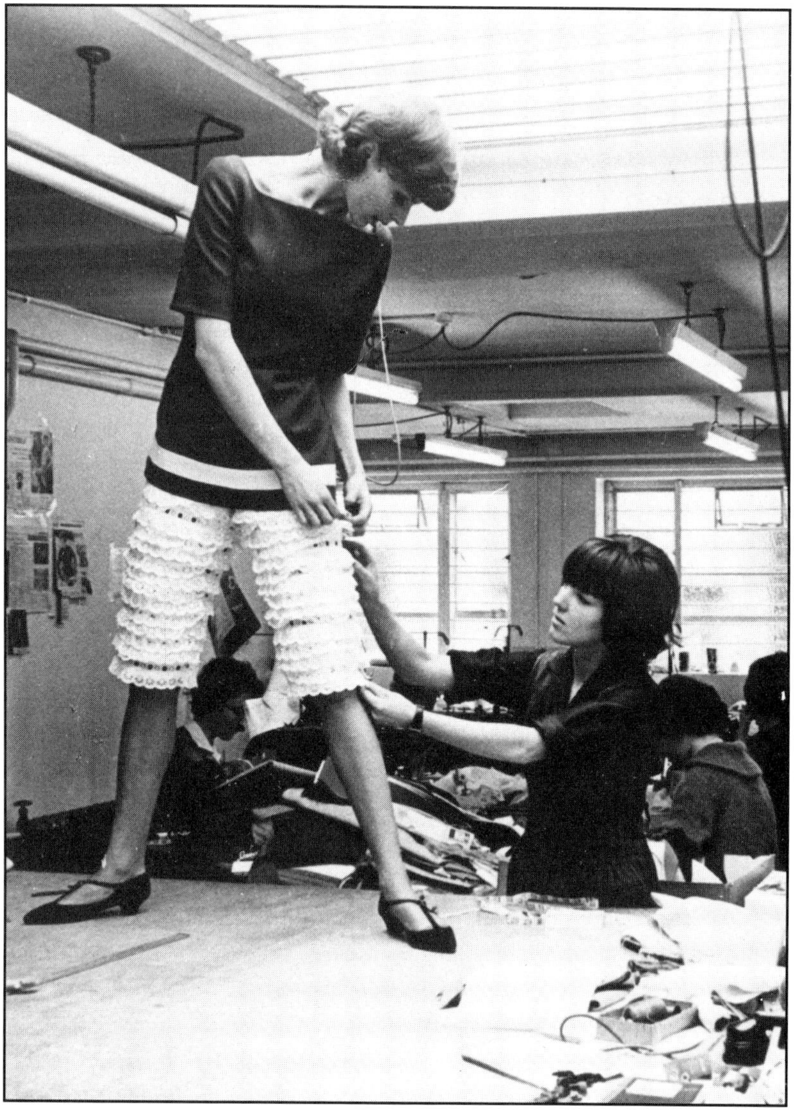

Above: A mini-skirted model pictured in King's Road, Chelsea, 1966. This road became the mecca for female fashion by the mid-60s

Right: Mary Quant (centre right) experimenting with a new design. By the mid-60s she had become the high priestess of the Mod look

colour photographs, in fashion features. As a result, fashion modelling and photography were transformed from the rather mundane jobs they had been into glamorous and lucrative careers. It was fashion photography which probably more than anything else helped to popularize the dream image of London as a 'Swinging City'. By the mid-1960s dozens of new photographic and modelling agencies were springing up in Central London. Young people from humble backgrounds did very well out of both professions, partly because the Mod cult was originally a working-class phenomenon and fashion editors felt that using them was a sure way of creating an 'authentic' look. Three of the most celebrated young photographers discovered during this period were David Bailey, Terence Donovan and Brian Duffy, all of whom were East End born and bred. One of the most famous models of the era was Leslie Hornby, better known as Twiggy, who was launched into stardom as 'the face of 1966' a few weeks before sitting her 'O' levels at Neasden High School for Girls in North London.

The fashion explosion in London also helped to fuel a boom in hairdressing. And following in the slipstream of Mary Quant's success was hairdresser Vidal Sassoon. Sassoon was an East End boy who had served his apprenticeship under leading stylist Teasie-Weasie. He came to dislike the grand and elaborate styles popular in the 1950s and, together with Teasie-Weasie, he developed a much more natural approach which they called the 'geometric cut'. Sassoon set up his own salon in Bond Street in the West End to exploit this new style, and by the early 1960s he had become very successful. Geometric styles perfectly complemented the unfussy clothes that Quant was designing and his cuts quickly became a great favourite with Mod girls. By 1966 he, too, was exporting his styles and salons to the United States. Sassoon had many imitators and London became dotted with a new generation of women's salons catering for the Mod look. Also, hairdressing salons for young men mushroomed all over the capital, many of them run by Italians offering a full range of Mod styles. Gone were the days when pioneer Modernists like Willy Deacey used home-made concoctions to get their hair looking right. Hairdressing for both men and women was now highly commercialized and was very responsive to the styles that young people wanted.

Just as the styles of dress and appearance of the early London Mods formed the basis of internationally famous fashions, so their musical interest provided a launch pad for dozens of rhythm and blues (R & B) groups to go on to international fame. The Modernists' early interest in modern jazz had by 1960 broadened to include authentic blues, soul and rhythm and blues music. This kind of music was hardly played or produced in Britain at all; it had to be imported, usually through records made by obscure American companies. The records of American artists like Muddy Waters, Chuck Berry and Howling Wolf quickly became collector's items and the more musically inclined Mods began forming bands and imitating the sounds of their heroes. The R & B music they created was a fusion of everything they had listened to, translated through the medium of the electric guitar which had become fashionable in the rock 'n' roll craze of the 1950s.

The most internationally famous London band of the Mod era was, of course, the Rolling Stones. Their first residency was at the

Craw-Daddy club in Richmond in 1963 where they played to packed audiences of local Mods. Yet although the Stones quickly became recording stars they lost much of their Mod following in the capital. Their appearance was too untidy for the liking of most Mods and their commercialized versions of favourite blues classics were seen as 'sellouts'. Much more in favour with fashionable London Mods were other home-grown bands like the Yardbirds – featuring lead guitarist Eric Clapton – the Kinks, the Pretty Things or Georgie Fame and the Blue Flames.

For a few years because of radio and television companies' opposition to pop music, bands like these were never heard outside a dozen or so London clubs. Their lyrics were sometimes blatantly sexual – expressing the more 'permissive' attitude of the younger generation towards sexuality – and the driving rhythms were disturbing to the untutored ear. However, the Mod bands on the London circuit were given a tremendous boost by two developments. In August 1963 a pop music television programme called 'Ready Steady Go' was given a prime-time early evening slot on ITV. Broadcast from a studio in Kingsway, Holborn, it was an instant success and featured bands on the London club circuit who were at the time virtually unknown outside the capital. A year later Britain's first pirate radio station, Radio Caroline, began transmitting from an old ship moored off the Suffolk coast. It was promoted by Ronan O'Rahilly, manager of one of London's top Mod clubs, the Scene club, and it plugged the Mod music that was being played in the capital. O'Rahilly's interest was blatantly exploitative: 'Youth was bursting out all over, there was a lot of money to be made.' Radio Caroline was quickly followed by Radio London, another pirate station which was geared to the capital's music scene. These outlets enabled London's Mod bands to reach mass markets and they produced a succession of hit

Teenagers on the set of 'Ready Steady Go' in the Kingsway Studio, Holborn. To begin with the audience was hand-picked from top Mods in Soho clubs. During its brief heyday in the mid-60s, the programme popularized the Mod music of the London clubs

records. The boom in record-buying which took off from the early 1960s onwards showed that teenagers were prepared to spend almost as much of their money on pop music as on clothes.

The two bands with the most distinctly Mod image and the biggest Mod followings in London to achieve commercial success were the Who and the Small Faces. The Who were the premier West London Mod band, and the driving force behind them was Pete Townshend, then a student at Ealing art college. They were, in fact, first called the Detours but in 1964 Townshend's friend Richard Barnes suggested a new name:

> There was this MC at the Oldfield Hotel dancehall in Greenford, where they played regularly, and he loved to have a little joke when introducing the group. He would say stuff like, 'And now I'd like to introduce the Detours – the Who? Never 'eard of 'em' and other assorted witticisms. I thought we could spike his guns for him. Townshend, incidentally, wanted to call the band the Hair. The next day he even suggested a combined name, the Hair and the Who, which sounded to me more like a pub than a group.

Having chosen their name, the Who obtained a residency at the Railway Hotel in Harrow where Townshend began smashing guitars – later to become the trademark of the band. Then their Mod manager insisted that the band dress in the latest Mod styles and introduced them to top Mods in the London clubs. Their first single was entitled 'I'm the Face' – the in-word for a top Mod – but it was their third release 'My Generation' which really launched them as a national phenomenon. The angry lyrics and crashing sound of this number brilliantly expressed the mood of rebellion against adult authority which lay behind the Mod cult.

The Small Faces, the most popular East End Mod band of the mid-60s

The most popular East End Mod band was the Small Faces. Most of the band were born and bred in East London and, as their name suggests, they too aspired to be 'top Mods'. By 1965 they were in the top twenty and their manager gave the band members an account at every boutique in Carnaby Street and £20 a week each to spend on clothes. They quickly developed a reputation for being Britain's best-dressed band which, in an era of narcissism, greatly contributed to their success.

Not only was there a remarkable growth of home-grown bands in London during the early 1960s; droves of young musicians eager to make it in to the big time came to the capital. They were lured by the growing fashionability of the London music scene and the fact that the booming pop industry was housed in London – for everthing from the recording studios to the factories manufacturing the new plastic discs was in the London area. Although the Beatles established themselves on Merseyside they moved from Liverpool to London in 1964, recording most of their music at the EMI studios in Abbey Road, St John's Wood. Their early music, however, was too melodic and their image too respectable for most Mods. Much more popular amongst the bands which gravitated to London were Zoot Money's Big Roll Band, who came up from Bournemouth, and the Animals who came south from Newcastle. Chas Chandler, former bass guitarist with the Animals, remembers coming to London in 1963:

> London was a huge magnet. The recording studios were in London – the only studio we had in Newcastle, if you put a drum kit in it, you couldn't get the drummer in. It was that small. You had to come to London. All the record companies were there, the music papers were there, they didn't review you if you hadn't played in London. Everybody got a nose bleed if they went north of Watford. We came down for ten days and stayed twenty-two years.

The mecca for the Mod music that most of these bands were playing was Soho. Many of the old jazz clubs like the 100 club became rhythm and blues venues for the new London bands. Those clubs most frequented by top Mods and top Mod bands were the Marquee, the Flamingo and the Scene in Soho. There were also a number of club venues for the new rhythm and blues music which were very popular with suburban Mods. The most important were the Eel Pie Island Hotel in Twickenham, The Craw-Daddy in Richmond and Klook's Kleek in Hampstead. And as the R & B clubs spread all over London so, too, did a new type of Mod haunt – the discothèque. Again this trend started in Soho at

The Mod look was smooth and sophisticated. These London Mods of the early 60s display some of its classic features: well-cut suits with narrow lapels, French hairstyles and Italian motor scooters

La Discothèque, which was the first London club to play records as opposed to featuring live bands. All-night dancing sessions at La Discothèque were quite common, and mattresses would be positioned around the side of the dancefloor for exhausted Mods to recover. By the mid-1960s the fashion for discothèques, complete with disc jockeys, had spread not only throughout London but across Britain.

Many of the Mods who went to the London clubs and discothèques had a hectic social life. Most attended clubs two or three times a week, and top Mods like Willy Deacey would often be out every night. He was able to afford this even though he only earned £6 a week as an apprentice printer. He remembers a typical week's social diary around 1964:

> Monday was Tottenham Royal, Tuesday the Lyceum, Wednesday the Scene, or maybe stay in and wash your hair, Thursday Tottenham Royal again (because it was our little hangout), then Friday night was 'Ready Steady Go'. It got difficult to get in on that so me and a friend used to get hold of an empty film can apiece and ride up and down the lift in the studios until it was time to go in, then we would just join the crowd. Then after 'Ready Steady Go' you'd go on to the Scene later. Saturday and Sunday was either a party or the Tottenham Royal, then the next week you'd start again.

Some Mods were only able to keep up this relentless social life by taking amphetamines which were then within the law. The pills were known to the initiated as Purple Hearts, French Blues, or Black Bombers. They could be obtained on prescription or bought for a few pence at many clubs. They gave Mods the extra energy to keep dancing into the small hours. Willy Deacey:

> We used to take Purple Hearts. They were legal then – in fact, my mum used to get them on prescription. They used to keep you going most of the night, but the only dodgy night was Sunday night because you were really tired then, so we'd take a handful and we'd be OK. There wasn't any dope around then so we used to take speed.

The obsessive pursuit of pleasure in their leisure time was in some ways a desperate over-compensation for the monotony and low status which many Mods had to tolerate in their work. For the Mod cult began as an essentially working-class phenomenon expressing the needs and wants of teenagers who were apprentices, factory hands, lowly clerks and shop assistants. The few serious studies of their sub-culture have shown that the central fact in most ordinary Mods' lives was boredom at work and at home. Many punters in London's night clubs were escaping into a glamorous dream world in order to fill their dreary working lives with exciting fantasies and memories. This was the only way that many could achieve the material success increasingly promised by the new consumer society of the 1960s. It was the tension between work (which was often loathed) and leisure (which was often seen as the main point of life) that gave the Mod cult much of its energy.

But by 1965 the hard-core of working-class rebels who had helped to create the Mod cult were beginning to lose interest in it. They had at first benefited from the commercialization of their style; Mod musicians and entrepreneurs were able to get rich quick and the records, clothes and hairstyles that the Mod punters wanted were much more widely available than before. However, by now the Mod style had become such a mass phenomenon that the original Mods found it difficult to identify with it. 1965 and 1966 were the peak years of Swinging London and, by this time, not only did a third of Britain's youth consider themselves to be Mods, but also the style had a sizeable international following. Every weekend Carnaby Street was filled with young Mods from the provinces or tourists from abroad buying up the latest fashions. By 1966, the year when Carnaby Street reached its height of fame, it was no longer frequented by London's top Mods – for they disapproved of this heavy commercialization of their culture.

The Mod scene had now become high fashion in London, and was being taken over by well-to-do people who lived in a different world to that of the original Mods. The styles of Swinging London were being 'sold' in articles, adverts and photographs which appeared in up-market glossy magazines and Sunday colour supplements. The smart metropolitan set became interested in the Mod style and began to adopt its fashions and mingle with its stars. From late 1963 onwards new exclusive London clubs opened where heirs and heiresses could meet the aristocrats of the pop world. The most popular amongst the young gentry were the Ad Lib off Leicester Square, the Scotch of St James near St James's Square, and the Cromwellian near the Cromwell Road in South Kensington. Here the new rich – pop stars like Mick Jagger and Roger Daltrey, leading designers like Mary Quant and Ossie Clark, top models like Jean Shrimpton, and fashionable photographers like Terence Donovan and David Bailey – rubbed shoulders with the old rich, forming a London jet set whose private lives filled the gossip columns of every newspaper. It was this image of young men and women from working-class backgrounds who'd made it to the top, mixing with the old rich that fed the myth that Swinging London was classless. Nobody was more keenly aware that this was an illusion than the original Mods, most of whom were still toiling away at their nine-to-five jobs often feeling cheated and upstaged by this 'take over' of their scene.

However, the main reason why the first generation of Mods were losing their commitment to the cult they had created was because they were now growing older. This simple fact of life, so important in explaining the changes of fashion in the pop world, also of course applied to the pioneer Chelsea set and the many other young people who had been influenced by the styles of Swinging London. By the mid-1960s many of these people were getting married, starting families and developing a different set of interests which often revolved around their new homes. As they moved on into married life they looked for a way of furnishing their homes that was compatible with their more sophisticated, 'modern' tastes. These fashion-conscious young people created a growing market for home furnishings, and the main style leader who moved in to exploit it was Terence Conran.

Conran had graduated from the Central School of Art and Design in 1950 and spent fourteen years persevering with his furniture designs in tiny attics and workshops in various parts of London. To make ends meet he had run several trendy soup kitchens in the West End. In 1964 he decided to open up a shop in Fulham called Habitat, selling modern, well-designed furniture and household goods at prices that most people could afford. Terence Conran:

> I'd always believed that well-designed things should be available to the whole population, that it shouldn't be an elitist thing. And I think this coincided with a lot of people who'd had further education coming through who were discontented with the way things were. The fashion revolution was just beginning – certainly, music was well on its way – and we wanted to provide home furnishings in the widest sense of the word to this type of person. There was beginning to be a little bit of demand for it – not a great deal – but you could feel the atmosphere of discontent. Most of the other stores weren't sensitive to change in society and they thought it was only a flash in the pan.

To begin with, Habitat wasn't very successful; the first shop only took £64,000 in its first year. But as more and more of the younger generation who had been influenced by the new styles of the 1960s moved into their own homes they created a mass market for the fashionable home-furnishings that designers like Conran were producing. By the late 1960s Habitat was booming, and on the way to becoming a nation-wide chain store. This transformation of the world of design completed the revolution in styles that was powered by Swinging London. What had begun as a rebellion of teenagers was now being incorporated into the new tastes and conventions of a consumer society.

The Swinging London scene faded after 1966 and from this time onwards the centre of gravity moved to the United States, especi-

Above: Terence Conran in 1952, posing with some of his early designs and constructions in an exhibition held in Simpson's of Piccadilly

Left: Interior of the first Habitat opened by Terence Conran in Fulham in 1964. As the 'Swinging London' set grew older and settled down, many turned to this shop for stylish household goods and fashionable home furnishings

ally to California. In the late 1960s California became the source of a new international counter-culture for young people, revolving around heavy rock music, drugs, mysticism, communal living and political dissent. The popularity of this hippie culture in Britain was, in part, a reaction against the commercialization of the Mod style. Many young people, especially those from a middle-class background, came strongly to dislike its concern with modernism, money and material success.

Post-1966 London would never regain the ascendancy it had enjoyed in the mid-1960s when, for a few years, it was a world style leader. Nevertheless, it did continue to be a style capital with successful fashion, design and music industries geared to the 'teenage' and 'young adult' markets. The life-blood of these industries were the styles of the new rebellious youth sub-cultures which, like the Mod phenomenon, would be commercialized and sold to a mass market. A similar process happened, for example, with the hippies, the punks and the New Romantics: they began in Britain as 'underground' movements in London but were quickly sucked into the capital's commercial machine – by now well established as *the* centre for British consumer industries directed at young people. This commercialization of style encouraged – as it always had – a greedy exploitation of the needs and wants of young people. However, there were also many positive features of the explosion of new styles in the capital. Most important, they helped to create a world in which there was greater freedom, choice and opportunity for young people, as well as consumer industries which more closely reflected their interests and tastes.

CHAPTER 3

The New Office World

The world of the office worker in London after the war was very different to that of today. The most striking feature of the late 1940s office was its formal and remarkably old-fashioned appearance. In the City it was a world in which bowler hats, rolled umbrellas and pin-striped suits still reigned supreme. Dundas Hamilton became a partner in a City stockbroking firm shortly after the war:

> The City was a very formal place; I mean, I came to work in a short black jacket and striped trousers and we all wore white shirts and stiff white collars. Everybody had bowler hats and rolled umbrellas because it was part of the uniform. In fact, it was so much a part of the uniform that when one of our young partners joined us my senior partner carpeted him because he wouldn't wear his bowler hat and he was thought to be improperly dressed. We also had a ban on the soft shirt or the coloured shirt, and if I'd worn a striped shirt and a soft collar people in my office would have said to me, 'Why haven't you got out of your pyjamas yet?'

Around a million Londoners were office workers just after the war. London's offices had been growing in importance for more than a hundred years, yet many of them still had an almost Victorian atmosphere. Dundas Hamilton remembers:

> The City offices in those days were much smaller than they are today, because businesses were smaller. Very few had central heating; most had gas fires. There was a Victorian atmosphere which came from tall desks with sloping tops where you could stand up and write if you wanted to. Or, if you wanted to sit down, you sat on a high stool. Virtually all the clerks were male. It was very much still the era of the pen-pushing clerk and the hand-written ledger.

From the 1950s onwards London's office world was to be transformed as it became the capital's fastest area of growth. This chapter tells the story of why this new office world developed and how it has helped to change the lives of millions of Londoners.

Previous pages: The new office world of the 60s with its preponderance of women, informality of dress and manner and open-plan setting, contrasted sharply with the old pre-war office, although (inset) the bowler hat remained part of the city 'uniform' for men until the late 60s

In the blitz hundreds of London's central offices had been damaged by fire and bomb blast, some of them being razed to the ground. Worst hit were the Barbican, Moorgate and the streets around St Paul's Cathedral, where almost every building was ruined. Something would have to be done to replace them. However, new office building was tightly controlled by the Labour government which came to power after the war. They saw London's office economy as a low priority in their reconstruction plan, and instead encouraged public housing schemes and factory rebuilding. Developers had to get an official licence before they were allowed to rebuild, and that was very difficult to acquire. Thus damaged buildings just had to be patched up rather than rebuilt.

The strait-jacket on new office building was tightened even more by controls which limited the height of buildings to 80 feet. This height restriction had its roots in an anachronistic piece of Victorian legislation, the London Building Act of 1894, which arose largely because of Royal objections to the 151-foot high Queen Anne's Mansions overlooking Buckingham Palace. Consequently, the architecture and skyline of London's business areas changed little for several years after the war. In the City, for example, the general height of office buildings was under 70 feet with many buildings actually only half this size. This created an office skyline which contrasted sharply with those of other major cities of the world, especially American cities like New York and Chicago, where great office canyons reaching up 400 feet were not uncommon.

In London, the old office way of life survived more or less untouched. Most office workers, especially in the City, were still men. They held a near monopoly of top jobs in the world of banking, insurance and finance, where the idea of senior women executives was almost unthinkable. If clients needed to be entertained for lunch then they would often be taken to that traditional and exclusive male preserve, the gentleman's club, which continued to thrive many years after the war. Dundas Hamilton remembers:

> When I became a partner in my firm I became a member of the City of London club. I lunched there virtually every day, sometimes taking business clients out. The food was very much the public school type, like roast beef and two veg. A particular delicacy was sausage and mash. This was the smallest and cheapest dish on the menu and, if you looked around the lunch room, you would see all the millionaires eating sausage and

The Prudential Insurance Company Headquarters in Holborn, pictured in the late 40s. Many offices had a Victorian atmosphere: this was still very much the era of the pen-pushing male clerk and the hand-written ledger

mash and thoroughly enjoying themselves. In the old days, of course, there were no women allowed inside the club, even as guests into the private luncheon rooms – partly, I think, because it was very much a male preserve and partly because the whole City was a male preserve. It was one of the rules of the club that people had to be principals in their firms, ex-directors or partners, in order to be eligible for membership and there weren't many women who were in this position.

Despite the fact that there were few women in the City, by the late 1940s they accounted for almost half of the office population in the capital. They had been making increasing inroads into office work for more than a hundred years. However, the vast majority were young and single, and they were massively concentrated in lowly positions like typists, telephonists, filing clerks and secretaries. This male domination of the office world was reinforced by rules which directly discriminated against women. They were based on the age-old assumption that the rightful place of women was in the home. The most famous was the marriage bar, which meant that women working in many banks and insurance companies, and for public institutions like the Civil Service and the London County Council were forced to resign on marriage. These rules had been relaxed during the war when married women had been recruited into offices as part of the production drive. But in the post-war years, when many married women became full-time housewives, the old discrimination returned, though often in a diluted and less formal way. Margaret Dent

Margaret Dent (seated fifth, left-hand row) worked for the Admiralty in Whitehall during and immediately after the war. She was one of many victims of discrimination against married women in the old male-dominated office

worked for the Admiralty in Whitehall during and just after the war:

> It was wartime when I got married and I had to stay on because they were short of staff, but it was very humiliating for I was immediately made a temporary member of staff and lost my pension rights. The whole attitude to women at that time in the Admiralty was that you were really only fit for making the tea and that you should be at home. You weren't taken seriously at all. I think if the attitude had been different I would have taken my career more seriously. But as it was I was glad to leave to get away from it all after the war, because the attitude to women there was terrible.

The 1950s and 60s were, however, to see the transformation of this old office world. The fabric of the capital underwent a sea change as new office blocks and towers sprouted up from bomb sites all over Central London, overshadowing the old Victorian heart of the Empire. The underlying force which powered this change was the enormous demand for office space in the capital, a demand which far exceeded the mere replacement of the office space lost during the war.

The big driving force behind this demand for offices in London was the growth of the City as the foremost centre of world finance. World trade boomed as never before in the post-war years and London re-asserted itself as the mecca of international money markets – it became the place to be in order to trade and invest most profitably. It established this dominance because it enjoyed better communications, greater expertise and fewer legal and tax restrictions on buying and selling than any other financial capital. The City was a particularly powerful magnet for banks and insur-

A view of Cannon Street taken from the top of St Paul's Cathedral in July 1956, showing the rebuilding of the City. In the 50s new offices sprouted up on bomb sites all over Central London

ance companies. They prospered greatly after the war, fuelled by the increasing amounts of international money attracted into the City. And as austerity gave way to affluence, banks and insurance companies benefited from billions of pounds worth of savings, pension schemes, insurance policies and life assurance to invest around the world.

As a result of this growth, the old bomb-damaged offices that had been patched up for continued use in central London were literally bursting at the seams. More office staff and more office space were desperately needed.

Added to this, London in the post-war years continued to attract company headquarters. Since the early part of the century, the increasing size and importance of companies like ICI and Shell had led them to establish their office headquarters in the capital, while their plants were scattered all over Britain and the world. This process was to continue apace after the war, as a host of multinational companies descended on the capital, some of the biggest of which were in the booming oil industry. And as the old giants like Shell expanded even more, they too were looking for new and bigger offices.

Also hungry for office space in London was the massive bureaucracy of the welfare state created by the post-war Labour government. The Civil Service, bloated by new departments, like the Ministry of National Insurance and the Ministry of Housing, needed much more office space than before the war. And the new nationalized industries, like the Coal Board and the Central Electricity Generation Board, were also establishing their headquarters in the capital.

The demand to have offices in London was given a further boost by the government's decision in 1946 to develop an unknown military runway at Heathrow to the west of London. As organizations grew bigger, so international trading in a developing world market was beginning to become more important. The new breed of jet-set executives who were emerging in London after the war needed to fly from one capital city to another. The new London Airport at Heathrow was the only airport in Britain which enabled them to do this.

But the extra runways and air terminals that London airport badly needed were not to be completed until the 1950s. At first, customs, inspection, immigration and refreshments were all housed in a short row of marquees and caravans. As late as 1950, a year in which 37,000 planes and over half a million passengers passed through Heathrow, there were still no permanent airport buildings. Also there was a desperate shortage of aircraft at this time, which meant that many old planes formerly used in the war were commandeered for service. Airlines had always geared themselves to first-class travel, equal to that of a trans-Atlantic liner; and the most luxurious planes boasted powder rooms, cocktail bars and promenade decks. In the austerity years, however, these standards were impossible to maintain and business flights from London Airport became incredibly primitive. Ron Bradburn was a young air steward at the time:

> For the passengers at Heathrow there were just two marquee-type tents – one was for the Customs and the other was for the passenger lounge and booking-in area. The primitiveness initially was such that, basically, all that was available was a few chairs in the passenger lounge, and a trestle table with a table cloth, an urn of tea and cups and saucers on it. The inside of the passenger lounge was also very primitive in furnishings; the floors were laid down with coconut matting. Later on they introduced a small bar where people could sit and have a drink before take-off. The passengers had to walk across duck-boards spread over muddy fields to get to the aircraft. At the end of the war there were very few planes around for commercial use, and so when BOAC wanted to start up very quickly to assist companies in London to do their business abroad once again, they had to use various military aircraft. The first ones that we used

The building of a new international London Airport at Heathrow gave a further boost to office development in the capital. Above left: The booking-in area, like practically everything else, was housed in a marquee tent in the early days, while (right) DC3s or Dakotas – pictured here – operated many business flights from Heathrow after the war. These planes had virtually no internal furnishings or facilities for passengers

were DC3s, commonly known as Dakotas. These were totally unfurnished inside. There were sixteen seats, virtually bolted to the floor, no curtains, no carpet – nothing like that inside. As far as the flying itself was concerned there was no pressurization and, because of this, the aircraft had to fly below 10,000 feet – above that there's no oxygen. When there was bad weather the plane was thrown about all over the sky and naturally many people were sick. In fact, we had what we knew as 'puke bags' or 'honk bags' for passengers to be sick in. Frequently I was sick myself trying to sort out soup, coffee, and God knows what, at the back of the aircraft where the tail was swinging backwards and forwards all over the place. The facilities for the passengers were minimal. There was a toilet on board at the rear of the aircraft and this was a straightforward chemical-type toilet, with no flush. And there was also a urinal 'pee tube' as we called it. This was a tube linked to the outside of the aircraft with a funnel on the end. You dangled what you had to dangle in the funnel, always being careful not to go too far because there was a suction element in the tube and, if you went too deep, the effect was like pulling a cork out of a bottle!

Despite these horrors the new London Airport at Heathrow provided a crucial international link for businessmen. This was the final key factor which made London the place where every major office wanted or needed to be after the war. This pent-up demand was to be unleashed on the capital when the new Conservative government – committed to growth in the office economy – took office in 1951. In three years they dismantled practically all the controls on office development in London. Building licences were abolished and so was the heavy tax on new office buildings.

Suddenly the bomb sites that spread across Central London became ripe for purchase and redevelopment in anticipation of an office boom. And, waiting in the wings to make a killing out of the boom, were hundreds of estate agents who were well aware of the great demand for office space in the capital. They quickly entered the office property market in a big way. The age of the property developer had begun.

The remarkable thing about the property developer was that he possessed little special skill or expertise in terms of knowledge of building and architecture. He was simply a 'fixer'. The property development system was at this time very simple and straightforward. A developer would obtain planning permission to build on a bomb site, arrange a bank loan to purchase it, then employ an architect and a builder to erect the office block on it. There was a small risk element in trying to find a company for the offices when they were completed. However, such was the demand for office space that some companies were prepared to take up and pay the lease even before the office was completed. Huge amounts were paid for leases, and developers like Joe Levy and Jack Rose became fabulously wealthy almost overnight. Jack Rose remembers how in those days a money-spinning deal could be clinched with just a few telephone calls:

> The demand for office space was insatiable and everyone was encouraging us to build more offices. When you saw a site for sale, you'd buy it sometimes on the same day and would be almost certain that you'd get planning permission and make a good profit on it. Once a site was on offer we'd ring up an architect (usually the same one) and he in turn would make a 'phone call to the planning authority. He would be told over the 'phone that he could apply for planning permission and told how many square feet of office space we'd be allowed on the site. Then we'd make a quick back-of-an-envelope calculation as to how much we could afford to pay for the site, and ring up and make an offer. What takes years today took days back in the 50s. And there were big profits to be made out of it. I left the army in 1945 with a gratuity of £18 and nothing else to my name. By the early 60s our company was worth £4 million. We weren't as big as many others – one of the greatest names was Lord Samuel whose company Land Securities was estimated to be worth, even in those days, £1000 million.

The idea was to pack as much office space as possible into a site. As it was a speculative venture, the building was completed as quickly and cheaply as possible in order to reduce the risks. Consequently, most offices had little ornamentation or individuality. The LCC gave planning permission for these new developments because modern offices were fashionable – the buildings of the future – and there was no conservation lobby to stop their onward march.

The result was a rash of rather ugly boxes. One classic example is the eight-storey high Woolworth House, by Jack Rose with architect Richard Seifert, completed in 1955 in Marylebone Road. Three years later Castrol House, also in Marylebone Road, became the first of a new style of concrete and glass office blocks. All of these buildings changed the character of the capital and Jack Rose now feels that many of them should not have been built:

> For the most part, they're nothing better than shoe boxes with glass windows in them! They should have been controlled by the planning authority who should have had a great deal better taste than they obviously had at the time. Wherever you see the boxes of that era they're being disguised – refaced and refurbished with what is now regarded as better taste. I don't believe in the preservation of a great deal of old property. Nevertheless, allowing a proper vista of St Paul's and other lovely and important buildings in London to go because of new offices was Philistine. Undoubtedly, the developers of that time didn't care. They weren't interested in what the buildings looked like – just how much profit they could make out of their building. When I look at the streets of London and at the buildings that were put up in that era, I'd say we made a muck of it.

But while the 1950s had laid the foundations of a fundamental change in the fabric of London's offices, it was only in the 60s that this all really came to fruition. Offices often took several years to complete and, as time went by, they were built higher and higher. It was really only in about 1962 that Londoners became aware for the first time of the extent of the transformation of London's skyline. In that year, for example, giant offices like the Shell Centre on the South Bank and the Vickers Tower on Millbank, both of them almost 400 feet high, were completed.

It was also at this time that there was another upsurge in demand for offices in London. Multinationals, especially booming oil companies, were expanding their operations in the capital. And banks were prospering as a result of the development of Euro-currencies like the Euro-dollar which attracted even more international money into the city. But the stock of bomb sites and derelict buildings which had been cleared and built on in the 1950s was now almost exhausted. So property developers began buying up Victorian offices, warehouses, churches and terraced houses, some of them in reasonable condition, and demolishing them to make way for new offices. During this mania for modernizing, almost every celebrated building in London came under threat from one scheme or another. For example, there were plans to demolish the Houses of Parliament, St Pancras Station and the whole of the southern half of Whitehall including the Foreign Office.

The early 1960s, then, were the era of 'monster schemes' in which many old buildings would be bulldozed to make space for huge office developments. Developers were able to plan ambitious schemes like these because they were now rich men with massive reserves of capital to draw on. Joe Levy, for example, was a millionaire as a result of property deals, and this wealth gave him enormous power.

The Euston Centre, the work of Joe Levy, was typical of this new 'monster' type of development. He secretly assembled properties and parcels of land in the Euston Square area in about 400 separate deals in the 1950s and early 60s. But he kept the whole operation secret. If he had made his plans public, the price of the remaining property he wanted to buy would have spiralled. Levy however was prepared to pay way over the odds for the last few properties he needed to complete the jigsaw of land required. He recalls:

> I'd spent more than ten years buying up all the land I needed, I had several millions pounds tied up in it, and it came to the point where there was one more house I needed to complete it. I think it was a Cypriot who owned it. It was a run-down old place worth next to nothing, but he was holding out for as much as he could get. The agent that was working for me made him some offers, and the price went up and up, but still he didn't want to know. So, one cold morning, I went down to see him myself. He refused to do a deal to start with but I said, 'There's no point in refusing, because the council will buy it compulsorily and then you'll get next to nothing.' We came to an agreement. I would give him £50,000. He wanted cash and all the documentation done immediately. I said yes and when it was done I asked, 'Have I made you a happy man?' He said, 'Yes, I'm happy now.' He was delighted with the deal, so I said, 'Now I'm going to tell you something that will make you very unhappy. If you hadn't sold to me now I needed your house so badly I might have paid you a quarter of a million pounds for it.'

By 1963 Levy had bought up the complete proposed site and the bulldozers moved in. The residential area of Euston Square was transformed into the Euston Centre, a mixed development mostly containing offices and shops, the centrepiece of which was a high-rise office block. It was to become the single most profitable office development in the world.

The LCC did little or nothing to stop these new office developments, for it was still broadly sympathetic to the idea of clean-sweep planning. In fact, it often helped large developers by making compulsory purchase orders, or by letting the property bought by developers remain unoccupied and decay, or by rehousing some of the displaced residents. 'Deals' were done with developers who in return would give the LCC small plots of land for road-widening schemes, which the office boom and the subsequent increase in commuter traffic was making very urgent.

The Euston Centre is a fairly typical example of this kind of deal. Joe Levy was allowed to build his offices in the way he wanted, on condition he handed over £1 million-worth of land he had assembled running through the site. The LCC used this free land to build the Euston underpass. And they gave property tycoon Harry Hyams permission to build the Centrepoint office tower, on a tiny traffic island off Tottenham Court Road, on condition that he donated an adjacent plot of land they needed for a new road scheme.

The buildings that office workers were heading for were not only changing in appearance. What went on inside them was also changing. A new style of mechanical office was emerging, which made greater use of labour-saving machinery. Some pioneering offices bought giant prototype computers. However, although

Below: Centrepoint completed in 1967. The LCC gave Harry Hyams permission to build this office tower on condition that he donated some land for a roundabout. Ironically, the roundabout was made virtually redundant by a new traffic circulation system before it was even finished

Right: Leo – 'Lyons Electronic Office' – was the first computer used for business purposes in the world. It was pioneered by J. Lyons of London in the early 50s

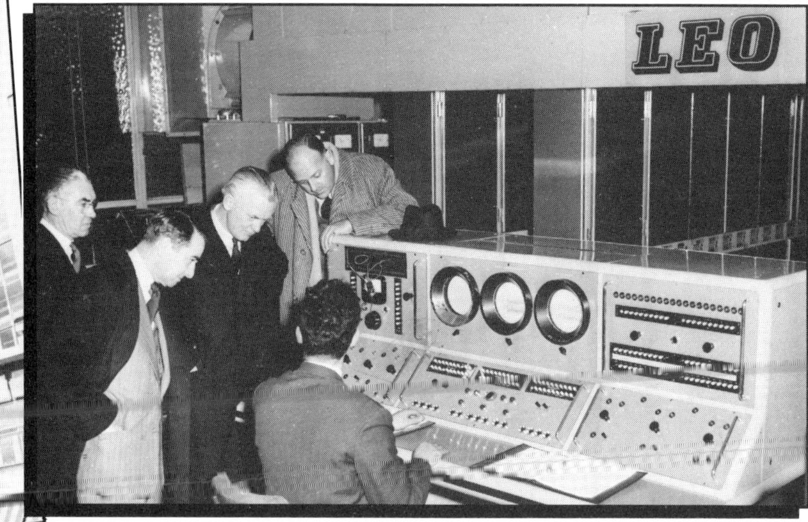

these early computers were bought to save time and money on clerical work, they were prone to going disastrously wrong. In the early 1950s J. Lyons of London became the first company in the world to use a computer for business purposes. One of the operators of this computer was Norman Beasley:

> Lyons decided that they would set about designing and building a computer themselves. They did, and they called it Leo. 'Leo' stood for Lyons Electronic Office. It was one of the first computers for commercial use, so nobody who was working with it really knew what to expect because no one had any previous experience of working with them. So, in a sense, it was very strange and sometimes things went wrong. We did work for other companies who of course didn't have their own computers then. One such was the Ford Motor Company. We did their payroll for them weekly and, of course, in those days it was cash in the packet on a Friday.
>
> One week it went wrong. The first we heard of it was when they told us that a clerk in the Treasury, who was responsible for putting money in the pay packets of the Ford workers, went to her supervisor and asked for a larger envelope. When the supervisor said, 'What d'you want a larger envelope for?' she replied: 'Well, I can't get this £478 in this one.' That was the first we knew that something had gone wrong.

Much more common in the mechanical office were small hand-operated machines like the typewriter. Typewriters had been used since late Victorian times but the increasing volume of work meant that now a great mass of them was becoming a central feature of every large office. The 1950s and early 60s saw the heyday of the typing pool; anything from ten to a hundred women would sit together arched over their typewriters all day. Anne

Serried ranks of typists in the Sun Alliance Insurance Company offices in the City in 1955. This was the heyday of the typing pool

Henderson worked in the ABC Cinema typing pool in Holborn in the late 1950s:

> It was a bit like being at school; there'd be about twelve girls in the pool, all sitting in rows with their typewriter on a desk in front of them. And the supervisor would be sitting in front of you like a school teacher would. It was very strict. You couldn't talk to the girl sitting next to you; you couldn't smoke and you couldn't eat. You would go up and collect your work in a folder, take it back to your desk, type it, take it back to the supervisor and then she would check it. If it was no good you'd have to collect it and do your mistakes. If that happened we'd all sort of moan and groan and pull faces. It was very boring work.

In fact, the development of a new generation of machinery in post-war offices meant that many of the old office craft skills became redundant. The ledger machine replaced the old ledger clerk. The dictating machine reduced the need for shorthand. The calculating machine cut down the time spent on sums and accounts, previously a source of pride for the clerk. And the first photocopying machines reduced the need for a lot of copying work. This spelt the end of the era of the pen-pushing male clerk who had occupied such an important place in the pre-war office.

For overwhelmingly it was women who were recruited to replace the male clerks and to do the new machine-based routine jobs in London's offices. By the early 1960s there were six women to every four men in offices in the capital. This was a complete reversal of the pre-war figures. Women were preferred to men for a number of reasons. The new office work was less skilled and complex than before and this type of repetitive work – according to the prejudices of the time – was thought to suit women far more than men. Also, in the days before the Equal Pay Act, women could be employed much more cheaply than men. Women office workers were paid around two-thirds the rate paid to men for doing the same job. Yet, despite this, more and more young women wanted to do office work. Many girls who were now enjoying a higher standard of education at London's new secondary modern and comprehensive schools saw working in offices as more comfortable and interesting than going into service or working in shops or factories.

The growing army of fashion-conscious young women recruited into offices became pioneers of a new, less formal office style. In the past, many women had had to wear sober coloured suits or even overalls in the office. Now they began to dress more as they pleased, confident that no one would reprimand them for fear of

Female office staff in the City in 1955. Until the mid-50s most women were expected to dress formally, clad in sober colours, at work. These rigid conventions were to be broken by the new generation of female office workers

losing their services – such was the demand for women office workers in London. Anne Henderson remembers:

> We used to wear very flared skirts with can-can petticoats underneath, and the more petticoats you had the better it was, so you'd be walking out dressed like someone on 'Come Dancing'. If anyone had tried to stop us wearing the clothes we wanted we would have changed our jobs – just left, gone down to the agency and said we'd lost our job; there was no sort of nastiness about getting the sack or saying that you'd walked out in those days. They'd have sent you off for a couple of other interviews the same morning; you'd be in another job by the afternoon. It was as easy as that!

The old formal office way of life was beginning to break down. The trendiest office-workers spent their lunchtimes jiving and twisting to the latest sounds at places like the Lyceum ballroom in the Strand. It opened from 12 to 2 p.m. on weekdays and hundreds of teenagers paid a shilling a session to escape into this noisy and exciting world of pop culture. One of them was Anne Henderson:

> We really used to look forward to the lunch hours because that was the time when we used to go jiving. As soon as the lunch hour came round we would rush into the loo, get more petticoats on, backcomb the hair up another four inches, put the black lines on the eyes, fourteen-inch points on the feet and we'd be straight over the Lyceum. Jiving at the Lyceum was really the highlight of our day because the work that we were doing was so boring and this was the one thing that we really

Above right: The lunch-time jiving session at the Lyceum Ballroom in the Strand, 1957. The trendiest office workers in Central London spent their lunch-breaks dancing to the latest sounds

Above: The late 60s were the era of the mini-skirted, 'dolly bird' secretary. To conceal their legs from ogling males a protective panel called the 'modesty board' (bottom right of picture) came into vogue

wanted to do. They would play records by Buddy Holly or Eddie Cochran or Bill Haley, and we used to dance with other girls. The girls didn't dance with the fellers because they used to stand around the side looking Teddy boy-ish. We'd rehearse elaborate routines beforehand and then we'd do all our steps and it would have to be absolutely perfect, and then we'd sit down and wait for the next record to come up that we'd practised to. Sometimes we might be ten or fifteen minutes late getting back to the office but usually nobody said anything.

By the early 1960s London had become the style capital of the world and the new look was to transform completely the whole atmosphere of London's offices. Many old Victorian conventions were swept away in a wave of informality of dress and manners. The late 60s were the era of the dolly-bird secretary with her miniskirt and heavy make-up. Companies which wanted to promote a glamorous image encouraged this trend by advertising for secretaries who were 'attractive, sophisticated and vivacious'. Temporary secretarial agencies like Girl Friday and Brook Street Bureau which sprang up everywhere often catered for this demand. Not all secretaries were of the dolly-bird breed, and not all companies wanted to employ them. Banks and insurance companies in the City remained far more traditional in their attitudes than the new advertising agencies and television companies in the West End. Nevertheless, it was during the 60s that the image of the secretary changed from being functional to glamorous, and most men were happy to encourage this trend. The dolly-bird secretary was, at one and the same time, the latest male executive toy – an office wife to tend to business and personal needs, and the greatest office status symbol that a man could possess. And the new office prosperity allowed many thousands of men in London, even down to junior management level, to enjoy their own secretary for the first time.

The dolly-bird secretary made the office a more erotic place than it had ever been before. One interesting consequence of this was the modification of office furniture to accommodate scantily dressed secretaries. Open-fronted desks and tables were becoming particularly fashionable in London but they now presented a new hazard for women office-workers. Many complained that men were ogling their legs and looking up their miniskirts as they sat at their desks. By popular demand, a protective panel called the 'modesty board' came into vogue in the 60s. Val Hill remembers how important they were to London's female office-workers:

> I worked in an office with lots of young girls all about my age and we all wore very short skirts – it would have been rather odd not to have done – and some of them were in very bright colours. This caused embarrassment for some of the men and excitement for others. Some of them couldn't stop staring at your legs. So we had modesty boards arranged on all the desks, which covered us in nicely – not just the front but the sides – and all in all we were quite satisfied with this; everyone was happy. It became one of the perks of a job; you not only asked for a rather good salary and an electric typewriter, but also modesty boards. And if there were no modesty boards then you might renegotiate the salary.

While most male bosses welcomed or at least accepted miniskirts, the fashion for trousers worn by women met a quite different response. Trousers in the office were still seen as a male prerogative and women who wore them were reprimanded for being untidy or unfeminine. However, trousers became popular amongst women office workers because they were convenient and warm in the winter. Inspired by the new liberalism of the 1960s and the beginnings of modern feminism, some young women staged small rebellions in offices all over the capital to win their right to wear trousers. Val Hill remembers one such revolt in the ATV offices in Marble Arch:

> Having argued that minis were acceptable as office clothes, we went on to trousers and trouser suits. I remember once a dread-

> ful hoo-ha about this, and memos being sent round saying that trousers would no longer be tolerated in the office worn by women. But, of course, men could always wear them. This made me very angry and everyone else very angry, and so we got together and said, 'Right! We'll all come in wearing trousers and see what happens.' Jobs were plentiful then so if we were dismissed it didn't matter too much, we'd just go next door and there'd be another office ready to employ us. So we all came in in trousers which I think were fairly smart, they weren't jeans. And nothing very much happened. There were a few tuttings but they seemed to be ignored. And a short while later we had another memo, individually sent to each one of us, which said it was all right for women to wear trousers in the office as long as they were not of a jean material or of a lewd nature. And we felt we'd won our case.

During the 1960s men's appearance and manners in the office were also changing quite dramatically. This was the time when more adventurous dressers wore shocking pink shirts and suede shoes to work. Out went the bowler hat, which had been an essential part of the uniform of London's office workers for many decades. It looked ridiculous with the longer hair styles and the more colourful ties, shirts and suits that were becoming fashionable. And in came not only more informal dress but also informal manners, as Dundas Hamilton remembers:

> I think in the 60s dress became less formal. I know I certainly hadn't worn my black jacket and my striped trousers for some time, and I gave up my bowler. I still carried my umbrella on wet days, but the lightweight suit that came in and the more relaxed type of dress – the soft shirt with the striped collar – all meant that the bowler never really looked quite in place any more. And when people's hair grew longer the bowler was really totally out of place. This was sad in a way because you used to be able to stand at the end of London Bridge and see what was like a colony of seals coming towards you, bobbing along in the morning – all identical black heads – that disappeared. I think also there was a greater relaxation in one's attitude and one's relations with staff. Previously one would call both one's equals and one's employees by their surname; if a person was on a par with you you called him Smith or Jones, or you might call one of your lowest servants Smith or Jones. In the 60s that changed. The christian name term, which had only been used for closest friends before, became much more wide-

spread. You started to call most people by their christian names and – surprise – your staff began to call *you* by your christian name, so the old disciplinarian rigidity faded out.

Of course, the ever-increasing number of office workers needed to eat at lunchtime. But the old eating places, like the Lyons Corner Houses with their sit-down meals and waitress service, couldn't accommodate this flood of workers. Also their rather formal atmosphere was becoming unfashionable. What the new office workers wanted was eating places that were quick and cheap and provided take-away food. To cater for them, hundreds of sandwich bars sprang up all over Central London, many of them started by Italians who were keen to run their own small catering businesses. Their initial growth was immediately helped by the invention of the luncheon voucher in 1955. This small daily perk for office-workers would buy a couple of rolls rather than a meal, and it quickly became common currency in the capital's sandwich bars.

This booming office world was generating much prosperity and a new office style for London, but it also brought with it one serious and immediate problem – traffic congestion. As office workers became more affluent they bought cars and drove to work, causing enormous traffic jams and parking problems. This was made worse by the emergence of the company car. From the early 1960s onwards more and more companies sought to avoid taxation by rewarding their managers with a new car rather than cash. London was quickly to become the company car capital of the world, as thousands of executives drove to work in cars that cost them nothing. Also, the outward sprawl of the capital's office economy into suburban areas like Croydon, Ealing and Wembley in search of cheaper sites, meant that traffic jams were not just confined to Central London. It seemed that the whole London area might grind to a standstill as rush-hour traffic led to terrible snarl-ups every morning and evening.

Traffic congestion in Holborn in the early 60s. The office boom caused enormous traffic jams and parking problems in Central London. This was one of the key factors which led to the government ban on office building in the capital in 1964

Since it was the government at both national and local level who were responsible for organizing transport systems and paying for expensive road improvement schemes, this was a problem which concerned them much more than individual companies. To try to improve traffic flow they introduced Britain's first traffic wardens and parking meters in Westminster, then quickly brought them in all over Central London in the early 1960s. What resulted, at least in the first few years, was a virtual war on the streets between motorists and traffic wardens. The anger and frustration of motorists combined with the inexperience and insecurity of traffic wardens, fighting to establish a new position of authority, was an explosive mixture. Tom Cook was one of London's first traffic wardens:

> In those days we often put ourselves over as fierce NCO types. We saw it as a war – us against them, us against the motorists. We didn't smile; we didn't want to know people or listen to their excuses; the attitude was to gaze into the middle distance. We were scared of being conned. If someone broke down and they were genuine we'd think, 'He's kidding.' The reason we

Tom Cook, one of London's first traffic wardens. In the early 60s war virtually broke out on the streets of the capital between angry motorists and inexperienced, insecure wardens

> did this, I think, was because we were something new, and I suppose we thought that we wouldn't be accepted, and that we had to take a hard line or people wouldn't take any notice of us. In those days lots of motorists didn't really accept our right to book them. If we'd had a policeman's uniform it would have been all right. But we didn't, so people were even more aggressive towards us than they'd normally be. We took minor assault as part of the job. I patrolled Soho, which meant that I was always going to have more than my fair share of problems, because it was quite a rough area in those days. I had an orange hit me on the face thrown from eight storeys up – walnuts, stones, the lot. Once I was cornered in an alleyway by a doorman about 8-foot wide and thought that was the end of me but he changed his mind after I thought he was going to do me in. Another time I was assaulted, I was booking someone and he threw me against a wall. As I landed on the floor a policeman came round the corner and I thought, 'Good, we'll prosecute!' But there was a traffic warden opposite and he came over and knocked the bloke out. We couldn't do anything about him then.

Meters and wardens helped traffic flow a little, but they made little impact on the great tide of cars flooding into London every day. So, in 1964, the new Labour government took dramatic action to try to get to the heart of the problem. It passed new legislation which at first banned, then strictly controlled, through a system of office permits, office building in the whole of greater London. This legislation, devised by Labour minister George Brown, became known as the Brown Ban. It put a brake on any more large-scale office developments in the capital until the end of the 1960s. A new era of office decentralization was beginning. Now most companies and government departments wanting to expand or to move away from Central London would have to move from the capital completely.

The government led the way by shunting about 50,000 jobs and several Civil Service departments hundreds of miles away to a host of provincial centres like Doncaster, Newcastle and Swansea. The private businesses, banks and insurance companies which moved away from London stayed much closer to the capital than government departments. They flocked to the South East, colonizing the outer suburbs and market towns in the Home Counties around thirty miles from London.

A new breed of office was rising in the green-field sites in these outer areas. They were office factories – bigger than ever before.

They often came to dominate the economies of small towns which became, in a sense, one-company towns. A typical example of this new office economy and office factory was the Sun Alliance company's development at Horsham, Sussex. The company moved here from the City in 1964. There were to be 1000 jobs in the Sun Alliance's new offices, but the vast majority were routine ones, for, in common with many companies who moved out at this time, they kept their head office and their top jobs in Central London.

Work at the Horsham office factory – like most other new office factories – was dominated by the computer. The Sun Alliance had decided to computerize all its policies and, as a result, the work of entire departments was geared to feeding information in and out of the computer. The new system required some skilled senior staff, and these were brought from Central London as part of the move. The skilled staff were practically all men, and women were overwhelmingly used to do the routine work, as computer clerks and punch-card operators, in the new office factory.

An old division of labour, in which men did all the highly paid career jobs and women did the lowly paid dead-end jobs, was being reinforced in these office factories. And as there were more unskilled jobs to be done, so more women were recruited to work in them. In the 1960s there was a big increase in women working in offices. Much of this was accounted for by mothers and housewives over thirty-five going out to work again. They were thought by office employees to be especially suitable for this type of work because they had low career aspirations and a reputation for being hard workers. Previously many suburban housewives had been confined to their homes but now many more went out to work either part-time or full-time in these office factories. The attraction was the fact that the offices were close to where they lived. Because travelling to work was easy, many women were able to fit in office work with the shopping and housework they were expected to do. They also had more time to spare, as housework itself was slightly less arduous and time-consuming now that they owned new labour-saving devices, like washing-machines, and smaller families and smaller houses were in vogue. After years of confinement in the home bringing up children, a job – however boring – was widely seen as a liberation by many of these older women workers.

But women who had once enjoyed careers felt frustrated at the routine nature of their work. Margaret Dent, formerly an executive officer in the Civil Service, became one of the Sun Alliance's first computer clerks at their Horsham offices:

> After I got married I never thought I would go back to work; it wasn't the done thing then. If you did it was very humiliating for the man because it was thought that your husband couldn't support you. Attitudes had changed by the 60s and when my children were all at school I thought I'd try for a part-time job. I longed to do something to get out of the house and I liked the idea of having my own money. But I had mixed feelings about the job I got. On the one hand, it was lovely to get away from the home and to earn my own money, and it was very convenient being so close. But, on the other hand, the work itself was rather boring. It took them about five minutes to train you for the job, just filling out computer cards, then they told you to get on with it. Nobody told you what the end product was, what you were doing it for. One longed to do something that one had been educated for.

The colonization of the market towns around London by office factories was to be overshadowed in 1970 by another property boom in the capital. The new Conservative government abolished many of the old controls which had slowed down office development since the Brown Ban. This triggered a renewed demand for office space in London which was swelled by a large influx of foreign banks that wanted to be close to the City money markets. But this time the developers and the planners would not have it all their own way. For there was a powerful conservation movement rising against them. The destruction of so much of the character of Victorian London to make way for anonymous office blocks had begun to cause some concern in the early 1960s. The most notorious episode which heightened awareness of what was increasingly seen as wanton vandalism against London's heritage was British Rail's unnecessary demolition of the magnificent Euston Arch as part of their plan to modernize Euston station and build new offices there. To begin with, the protests were voiced by a few architects or literary figures like John Betjeman, but by the early 1970s the conservation movement had become genuinely popular and radical, because it now aimed not just to protect threatened buildings but also communities that were threatened by the planners. There was a growing anger amongst ordinary Londoners against grand redevelopment plans which threatened to steamroller their communities. It had happened during the 1960s in places like Euston Square where tenants, small businesses and shops were dispossessed and dispersed with little compensation. Now people were determined that this kind of thing should not happen again and they united to resist new developments.

Above right: The magnificent Euston Arch, completed in 1837 as the entrance to the first trunk railway line in the world. It was demolished in 1962 as part of the modernization of Euston Station, which involved the building of new roads and offices

Above: Demonstration against the plan to modernize Covent Garden in the early 70s. This campaign was a triumph for the conservation movement in the capital: subsequently developers had to show much more respect for historic London than they had in the past

The most fierce conflict of community activists against developers and planners came with the battle to save Covent Garden during the 1970s. Much of this Dickensian and densely populated area was in a badly run-down state containing tenement slums and empty warehouses. When the long-awaited removal of Covent Garden market to Nine Elms was finally scheduled to go ahead in the early 70s, the GLC came up with an ambitious development plan to replace the old buildings with new offices, shops and homes for displaced residents. But those who lived and worked in Covent Garden, which included a hotch-potch of printers, publishers, violin-makers, plus many actors based in the area's eighteen theatres, didn't want to move and were determined to maintain its old character. They formed the Covent Garden Community Association to campaign against the redevelopment. One of its leading figures was printer John Toomey:

> A group of local people heard of this horrific plan. We got together and a public meeting was called in the Kingsway Hall, and that is how it all started on 1 April 1971. And to our amazement 600 people turned up for that meeting, so it gave you the feeling that people wanted to keep Covent Garden. They didn't want it turned into office blocks and sky scrapers, and have conference centres put up in its place. Well, we got the people together and we marched; we held candle-lit processions over

> to County Hall; we went to Parliament; we met MPs – the Minister of the Environment and people like that – to fight our case for Covent Garden because we loved Covent Garden.

The campaign was a triumph for the conservation movement in the capital. The government bowed to local pressure by listing many of the existing buildings in Covent Garden, and the GLC scrapped its redevelopment plan. The campaign proved to be a turning point in new office-building in London for, after this, developers would be more restricted in their scope and would have to show more respect for historic London than they had in the past.

This crusade against new offices coincided with the world recession in 1973, which in turn put a brake on any spectacular office development of the sort which happened in central London a decade earlier. The recession in fact meant the end of some of the taken for granted features of the office boom years. A number of property development companies went bust due to the dramatic increase of interest rates. These companies lived off borrowed money and suddenly the interest on their huge bank loans became too big to pay back. No longer was it possible for an individual to become a property tycoon almost overnight. From now on, banks and pension funds moved in to control what was seen as a very high-risk business.

The era of the dolly-bird secretary also came more or less to an end. The recession forced many companies to make cuts, and one of the first targets was the personal secretary – the gift of the 1960s to junior and middle management. In Central London by 1980 a secretary was costing £8000 a year just for the office space she occupied, even before she was paid a salary. From the late 1970s onwards apart from the office elite, most managers had to share their secretary with other colleagues. Also at this time new equal rights legislation meant that all the sexist adverts for attractive secretaries had to stop.

Finally the 1960s saw the end of the tradition of keeping head offices in Central London, even when companies moved out to cheaper sites. As more and more offices left Central London to avoid exorbitant rent costs, increasingly they economized by taking everything with them. Most gravitated to the South Western corridor, beginning in Hammersmith, passing through Ealing, and following the course of the M4 to Reading and beyond. Rank Xerox, ICI and British Aluminium were just three of the major companies that took this route in the 1970s. Here they built a new generation of electrical and electronic offices, complete with the latest computer technology to save labour costs.

Yet, despite these changes, Central London has remained a thriving international office capital, enjoying a great concentration of head offices and top office jobs. The great wealth generated by this office economy continues to shape the character of much of the capital, though now it colonizes older areas as often as it rebuilds them. A classic case of this is Covent Garden. Ironically, though the original fabric of Covent Garden remains intact, it was not to be kept for the people who had fought to defend their 'village' against office workers and shoppers. The historic architecture and atmosphere of Covent Garden became more and more fashionable, and increasingly colonized by chi-chi shops and expensive wine bars and bistros. Sandwiched between the prosperous offices of the City and the West End it has thus been drawn into the orbit of London's new office world, becoming very popular with the trendy young generation of office workers during their lunch hours. All this is a far cry from the gentleman's club and the formality of old office London. But it is striking testimony to the continuing prosperity of London's new office world.

CHAPTER 4
Moving Out

On 20 April 1959 there were scenes of great municipal splendour in Stevenage as the Queen unveiled a commemorative plaque and officially opened the new town centre. Yet, although this event was taking place in a new town thirty miles away from the capital in the middle of Hertfordshire, most of the cheering, flag-waving inhabitants were Londoners, who had actually been born and bred in places like Tottenham, Hornsey and Islington. For many of them, this was a symbolic moment when their new identity as people of Stevenage finally became established.

Alf Luhman had been one of the new town's earliest residents, having moved from Tottenham to Stevenage in 1952. He remembers the Queen's visit:

> I think it meant to Stevenage that at last we were recognized. The town was no longer a building site, but a real town and the Queen had come and granted us a charter so to speak, and

Previous page: A proud London couple inspect their new home in Harlow New Town in the early 50s

The Queen officially opening the Stevenage New Town centre in 1959. For many of the Londoners who had moved out to the new town this was a symbolic moment: their identity as people of Stevenage was now fully established

> everybody in Stevenage who had worked so hard to see the town grow felt that it was an honour. At that time we were still very much Londoners, we were visiting at least two or three times a month and we used to go up at weekends to see our family. But with the Queen coming I think we started to throw that off.

During the post-war years more than a million Londoners moved out to set up home in new towns, market towns and villages all over the Home Counties. While the 1920s and 30s had seen a mass migration from the centre of London to sprawling suburbs around the capital, the new exodus involved moving out much greater distances. After the war huge tracts of the South East between twenty and fifty miles from the capital were colonized by Londoners and transformed as they were sucked into the orbit of London's economy and social life. This chapter tells the story of how London moved out.

At the heart of this post-war exodus lay the fact that London had grown too big, too fast; something had to be done to halt its expansion. After its spectacular growth in the Victorian era, the population of Greater London increased by a further 2 million during the inter-war years, as droves of jobless people migrated from declining industrial regions in South Wales and the North West to work in the capital's booming industries. By the outbreak of the war London housed over 8½ million people, but this concentration of population was creating serious problems. Worst affected were the inner areas where over-crowding, slum housing, pollution and disease were rife. The outer areas suffered from ugly suburban sprawls, loss of valuable agricultural land, and commuter traffic jams which, though less dramatic than the poverty of life in inner London, were attracting a growing chorus of criticism by the early 1940s. On top of this, London bore the brunt of wartime destruction; in the central areas nine out of ten homes suffered some sort of bomb damage. During and after the war most people believed that the most sensible solution was to disperse London's congested population and build new homes for Londoners away from the capital.

The first great impetus for this outward movement came from the government. It appointed Patrick Abercrombie, Britain's most eminent planner, to draw up a master plan for the dispersal of London's population. Professor Abercrombie came up with the Greater London Plan, published in 1944, which became the blueprint for the post-war reconstruction of the London area. He envisaged a million people moving out in ten years as part of a mas sive decentralization of population and industry from central and suburban London. The thrust of the plan was to build a ring of ten new satellite towns, twenty to thirty miles away from the capital, each containing between 30,000 and 60,000 people. Abercrombie's plan was seized upon by the idealistic Labour government, which triumphed in the 1945 election on the promise that it would build a better Britain with improved housing for all. The plan offered an immediate way of tackling London's housing crisis and a vision of a new future for ordinary Londoners. This was to be the heyday of state intervention and social engineering on a scale never seen before in Britain. Prime Minister Clement Attlee appointed Lewis Silkin as chief of the new Ministry of Town and Country Planning, with a brief to implement the new town policy as quickly as possible.

The site that was destined to be the prototype for the first generation of new towns was the small, thriving agricultural town of Stevenage. It was recommended in Abercrombie's plan and was particularly attractive to planners because it was situated on the Great North Road and on the main London to Newcastle railway line, and thus possessed excellent communications. Early in 1946 there were rumours amongst locals that Stevenage was to be chosen as the first new town. These were confirmed when in April the postman delivered letters informing 178 residents that their property was to be compulsorily purchased by the Ministry of Town and Country Planning.

The government had assumed there would be little resistance to the new town plan, but they were quickly proved wrong. What became known as the battle for Stevenage was about to begin. Angry locals, including many farmers who wanted to keep Stevenage as it was, formed a militant Residents' Protection Association. Lewis Silkin first tasted the strength of local feeling when he visited Stevenage on 6 May 1946 to explain to locals why it had been chosen for what he called 'a daring exercise in town planning'. He was met by thousands of protesters, and the town was festooned with posters saying 'HANDS OFF OUR HOUSES!' and 'NO! NO! MR MINISTER!'. At the meeting he responded to barracking by replying 'It's no good your jeering! It is going to be done!' Meanwhile, outside the Town Hall, saboteurs put sand in the petrol tank of Silkin's chauffeur-driven Wolsey and let the tyres down.

Both the government and the Residents' Protection Association were now set on a collision course. If Silkin backed down then the whole new town policy would be in jeopardy. On the other hand, the homes and businesses of the Stevenage residents were at stake. The government's strategy was to rush through a New

Lewis Silkin (walking through gate, centre front) in Stevenage, May 1946, to speak to the locals about the government's decision to turn this rural backwater into London's first new town. In the protest which followed, saboteurs let down the tyres and poured sand into the petrol tank of his chauffeur-driven Wolsey

Towns Act so that by August their policy became law and Silkin issued a draft order designating Stevenage as London's first new town. The residents responded by demanding their right to a public enquiry to hear objections to the plan. The enquiry heard a unanimous rejection of the new town, and as there was no minister present to defend the government action it was assumed that the locals had won. However, the simple truth was that the government was so convinced its master plan was in the public interest it felt no need to justify its actions to the locals. On 11 November 1946 Stevenage New Town was officially designated and the Stevenage Development Corporation, a government-appointed body, was established to build and run it for the public good.

The locals were outraged and one of them, Jack Franklin, won a blaze of sympathetic publicity by venting his anger in a particularly witty way:

> A friend of mine coined the word 'Silkingrad', obviously after the Minister [Lewis Silkin] and we thought this was rather witty. And the three of us got together, two doctors' sons and myself, and we manufactured fake signs for the railway station and fake signposts saying 'Silkingrad'. We made these out of hardboard and cardboard and took a lot of trouble with them and then, one moonlit night in December (it was very frosty and a bit of snow was about) we put these signs up in the station. It was rather like a military operation, and we glued them on with aircraft glue and they looked quite official. I was on the top of a ladder putting a large Silkingrad sign over the booking hall when the local

To express their anger at the dictatorial fashion in which Silkin designated Stevenage a new town in 1946, locals put up signs saying 'Silkingrad'

bobby turned up. I knew him quite well and he just wandered up, and I called down from the top of the ladder 'Is your wife a good cook?' On being told that she was I said, 'If you look in the back of our van I think you might find a brace of pheasants.' That was the end of that. And we got these signs up and we'd tipped off the press and they came down posthaste next morning and it got in the national press in forty-eight hours. Even got in the American press!

Jack Franklin's father, a wealthy local farmer, was more serious in his fight against the government, and he took it to the High Court. In February 1947 the order designating Stevenage as New Town was quashed because it had overridden local objections, but the celebrations of the locals were short-lived. For, within a month, the government had appealed against the decision and won the battle for Stevenage.

So Stevenage New Town was built after all. Yet it was only because this was an era of strong central government when planners enjoyed immense power that the new towns project was able to get off the ground. In the next two years London's other new towns were designated and, although locals were often unhappy about their future, there was no other resistance movement like that which emerged at Stevenage, for opposition to the government was now seen as futile. The new towns to be built were, in order of designation, Crawley, Hemel Hempstead, Harlow, Hatfield,

Welwyn Garden City, Basildon and Bracknell. In fact only two of these – Stevenage and Harlow – were originally selected in the top ten suitable sites for development into new towns. The ones which escaped this fate were Redbourn and Stapleford in Hertfordshire, Ongar and Margaretting in Essex, Meopham in Kent, Crowhurst and Holmwood in Surrey and White Waltham in Berkshire (see map page 101). They were able to continue as semi-rural backwaters not because of the strength of local opposition but because government officials eventually found them to be unsuitable.

If the battle for Stevenage was over, another was just beginning – actually to build the fabric of the new towns. At Stevenage no permanent houses were built for over three years by the Stevenage Development Corporation. The only sign of activity was an information office and a team of surveyors who scurried around in landrovers inspecting the lie of the land. It had originally been predicted that by the beginning of 1951 Stevenage New Town would be housing over 30,000 Londoners, but when the time came the first family were still waiting to move in. There was a similar dearth of house-building in the other new towns. The reason for this was lack of government money for big housing projects due to Britain's heavy post-war debts, and a shortage of building workers and materials.

In fact, until the early 1950s most working-class Londoners moving out of the capital moved not to new towns but to new council estates like Oxhey and Boreham Wood in Hertfordshire, and Debden and Harold Hill in Essex, all built by the LCC. They were similar in look and design to the inter-war cottage estates, such as those in Dagenham, but they enjoyed advantages like upstairs and downstairs toilets (insisted upon by the new Labour government), and were bigger and better than before. Their main drawback was the fact that they were situated fifteen to twenty miles from the capital, which for many people meant a long and expensive journey to work into London each day.

Abercrombie strongly opposed the building of these new 'out-county' estates, on the grounds that they were perpetuating the inter-war problems of suburban sprawl and class segregation. His vision, shared by many other planners and politicians in the post-war years, was much grander and more utopian. The twin ambitions for the new towns, which made them unique, were that they should be self-contained and balanced communities. Self-containment meant that both homes and jobs would be provided so that the newcomers could avoid the tiring and time-consuming business of commuting to work. Social balance involved attracting a wide range of different classes into the towns; workers would live next door to managers, and they would share the same schools, churches and community centres.

This ideal of a new community was rooted in the writings of Victorian social reformer Ebenezer Howard, who advocated the building of small garden cities in the countryside where people could enjoy the benefits of rural and urban life. He believed that moving people out to garden cities would inspire a moral and spiritual regeneration that was impossible in places like London, where poverty, disease and crime were endemic. This vision of social harmony in the new towns was embraced by post-war governments and by the staff of many development corporations twenty years after Howard's death. It was a curious mixture of utopian socialism and a rather backward-looking and paternalistic conservatism, well summed up by the Chairman of the Stevenage Development Corporation when he declared in 1947: 'We want to revive the social structure which existed in the old English villages, where the rich lived next door to the not-so-rich, and everyone knew everybody.' The contradictions in this philosophy were to emerge in the 1950s when house-building and industry in the new towns really took off.

Self-containment in the new towns meant providing an abundance of jobs for those who lived in them. As a result, the towns vied to attract up-and-coming industries, often in engineering and electronics, in order to establish a prosperous economic base. Many of these growth industries did indeed gravitate to the new towns, some of them moving from London, but they tended to employ a high proportion of skilled workers. This in itself contradicted the original aim of attracting a perfectly balanced community, for the majority of newcomers were drawn from the skilled working class. This imbalance was reinforced by the fact that eligibility for a council home in the new towns was not determined by Londoners' housing needs. To get a council home you first had to get a job, and the types of job which were available to Londoners excluded most unskilled and semi-skilled workers and their families who were often living in the worst housing conditions.

Although the new towns did not recruit the poorest from the capital, housing conditions were generally so bad for working-class Londoners after the war that practically everyone who moved out found their new homes comparatively luxurious. Most of the new town homes were either in short terraces or semi-detached, and tenants particularly favoured the privacy and convenience of having the whole house to themselves. Many were enjoying a bathroom, a garden and their own front door for the first time. Alf Luhman remembers:

Conditions were bad in London; we had no water at all and we used to share the tap with the landlady. We had to use the local baths for our own baths. There was a garden but we weren't allowed to use it. There was no hope of bringing the children up under those conditions, they were growing up and getting bigger and as they got bigger so the conditions became worse automatically. We were desperate, so desperate in fact that because we were unable to be housed by both the council and the LCC, we decided the best thing to do was to up sticks and go to Australia. So I got myself a job and was ready to go out to Australia to ensure that the kids had a decent home. Well, at that time there was this hoo-ha with the Silkingrad business. I think it got in the news, and I said, 'Well, if they're going to build a new town in Stevenage thirty miles away I'll try it.' So, of course, I got on the train and came down here and got a job and was told that if I worked here for three or four months I'd get a house. And it was ideal; exactly what I wanted. So we sent all the papers back to Australia House and decided to come to Stevenage.

Anne Luhman:

I was thrilled with the home, it was really lovely – to think I had my own sink, my own bathroom, two toilets, one up and one down. I felt I was on holiday for months and months; the children thought it was great. There was a green dell at the side of us, and they just ran round and round. They felt free.

Below left: Anne Luhman with her children, pictured outside her late 40s' home in Tottenham. The flat lacked the most basic facilities, like running water or a bathroom. Her new home in Stevenage (below), where she moved in 1953, was so luxurious after Tottenham she felt as if she was on holiday for many months

Despite the fact that Londoners were very pleased with their new homes there was much criticism of the modern design of many house interiors. These complaints arose from the crusading work of development corporation architects who were often inspired by a mission to bring simple, modern and functional design to ordinary families, and rescue them from 'bad taste' and class-bound Victorian traditions. Some homes, for example, were built in an open-plan style, with one large room downstairs replacing the old division between a parlour at the front of the house, used for best occasions, and a living- and dining-room for everyday use at the back. The parlour was seen as a symbol of class snobbery inherited from the Victorian middle classes, and was dispensed with as a pretentious waste of space.

However, a study of Harlow residents by sociologist Judy Attfield has shown that this type of innovation was often strongly disliked by families moving out to the new towns who saw a parlour for display purposes as part of the natural order of things. The response of many people was to take the furnishing of the new sitting-cum dining room where they spent most of their time, much more seriously than before, for they were now constantly on show through the large picture windows at the front. The favourite status symbol of the 1950s was the cocktail cabinet – which often remained empty because the proud owners could not afford to stock it – cheap three- or even five-piece suites, and television sets and carpets, most of which would be bought on hire purchase.

While the attempt to uplift residents to open-plan design met with some disapproval, the more important new town goal of integrating people from different classes aroused a much deeper resistance. It was quickly discovered that fundamental divisions of language-use, culture and interests between the classes could not be wiped out by a few plans emanating from Development Corporation offices. It was originally thought that the simplest recipe for class-mixing was to build larger houses for the middle classes in the same neighbourhood or even the same street as smaller houses for the working classes. However, by the mid-1950s it was clear that managers were simply not prepared to live next door to workers. Bigger houses in 'mixed' streets and neighbourhoods were very hard to let, and some of them remained unoccupied. In contrast, where a more exclusive one-class neighbourhood was developed, often next to a golf course or beauty spot it quickly took off as a desirable place for professional people. Very soon the idealism of development corporations in new towns like Stevenage and Crawley bowed to market forces, and neighbourhoods were more and more custom-built for different classes. From the

Above: Open-plan interior of a 50s Harlow New Town home. This innovation was often disliked by working-class families, who preferred the old-style parlour at the front for best and a living-cum-dining room at the back for everyday use

Above left: The Hertfordshire County Mobile Library on an occasional visit to Stevenage in the early 50s. At this time the town suffered from a lack of social and recreational facilities

mid-1950s onwards choice plots of land were sold to private builders who put up snazzy new homes. As home ownership amongst the middle classes boomed this was becoming the most effective way of attracting professional people into the new towns. Even then, some of the better off chose to live in picturesque nearby villages, rather than live in the new towns themselves, which were viewed by many as characterless and boring places.

The working classes, having less money, did not enjoy the same degree of choice as to where to live, but even they helped to re-inforce further social segregation. More affluent and ambitious workers would, after a few years, often move to rent brand new or bigger houses in newer neighbourhoods. As time went on old neighbourhoods with lower rents, like Bedwell in Stevenage, became magnets for less well-paid workers and their families, and some of them earned the reputation of being problem estates. Thus by the late 50s there was a general realization that the dream of a truly classless new town community would never come true.

One of the beliefs which underpinned the movement to mix different classes was the assumption that workers and the communities they lived in would greatly benefit from the leadership and organizational skills that only professional people could provide. The new-town experience was to prove this theory spectacularly wrong, because in the 1950s there was a flowering of community activism by working-class people in their one-class neighbourhoods. This activism stemmed from an almost complete lack of social facilities in the new towns in their early days. The Conservative Party, which returned to office in 1951, had little commitment to state-run projects like the new towns, and they pruned their budgets. As a result, although house-building could continue, there was little money available for anything else, like schools, hospitals, shopping and community centres, roads,

A cavalcade of cyclists, motor cyclists and pedestrians hold up traffic in Stevenage in 1954 as part of a campaign for the building of a footbridge across the A1 which passed through the town. The residents of Stevenage were particularly militant in demanding basic amenities in the 50s

transport, street lighting and so on. The first residents were shocked to find themselves marooned on a gigantic building site which in the winter months turned into a sea of mud. They had to walk miles to the nearest shops, pubs and schools. As pioneer resident Michael Cotter put it, 'I felt as if we had been dumped on the side of a hill and left to our own devices.'

This lack of basic amenities and things to do was one of the key factors which led to the much-publicized sense of loneliness and isolation dubbed 'the New Town blues', felt by the first generation of newcomers. A few – less than one in a hundred – returned home, but the majority decided to stay and fight for better conditions. The most militant and successful Tenants' Association emerged in Stevenage, once again, where they mounted a series of demonstrations, marches and petitions to get things done. They fought for a school, a hospital, community centres, street lighting, better bus services, and the building of the Stevenage by-pass, to prevent the many serious accidents which resulted from the A1 running through the town. One celebrated cause was their campaign for a traffic-free town centre which, when it was completed in 1959, was the first pedestrianized shopping precinct of any size in Europe. Out of all these struggles emerged a strong community spirit. Michael Cotter went on to become one of the leaders of the Tenants' Association in the 1950s:

> We were determined to make it work. We had a nice home at last, just what we had always wanted, so we weren't going to give that up; we decided to fight for everything we needed. We weren't educated, we never spoke publicly, never had any dealings with people in authority; we just learnt it all as we went along. We discovered fairly early on it was no use being soft, they would not take any notice of us, so we started to take a hard line. There were no primary schools, no buses, no shops for miles. We didn't want it all in a few years' time; we wanted it

A typical kitchen in a Harlow New Town home of the mid-50s. The new towns provided a high standard of housing for the Londoners that moved out to them

> now. We organized marches, mass meetings down in the town hall, all sorts of demonstrations. There was a great spirit that brought everyone together then, and the women were fantastic – they backed their husbands come hell or high water.

By 1959 the first generation of new towns had come of age. Despite the failure to realize some of their original ambitions most had achieved a great deal. They had established a strong foundation of successful industries; they offered more than enough jobs to satisfy those who lived in them; and they provided a high standard of housing, better than anything that most Londoners who moved out had ever known before. On top of this, they were by now beginning to make handsome profits from the renting of factory and office space to firms, and were proving to be one of Britain's most successful nationalized industries. More than 120,000 people were now living in London's overspill new towns and most of them, like Alf Luhman in Stevenage, were pleased they had moved out:

> It was the finest move we ever made; we had no regrets. We were able to raise our children in very good conditions. We had to struggle for things but when we got them they were brand new. We had brand-new schools and, again, we were fortunate because we were involved and helped to choose the headmasters and the teachers. And we were on the governing bodies and what have you, whereas if we'd been in London you never had that sort of opportunity. It all became a very close-knit family in those days, and everything we did was for the benefit of our kids. To us that was the most important thing.

In addition, another 30,000 Londoners had been exported to what were called 'expanded towns' all over Britain. These were towns which, under the 1952 Town Development Act, came to an arrangement with the LCC to rehouse Londoners in return for government grants for public housing and industry. This initiative, which aimed to supplement the new town scheme, was very attractive to declining agricultural areas, and several East Anglian towns, like Haverhill, Thetford and Bury St Edmunds, received many families from the capital. Some Londoners went even further afield, and the most distant places which participated in the scheme were Swindon, Plymouth, and Bodmin in the South West, and Grantham and Gainsborough in Lincolnshire. These expanded towns were planned like miniature new towns, and although they experienced some teething problems, most of the Londoners who moved out to them had few regrets.

Yet despite this planned movement out of London it fell far short of Abercrombie's target for the decentralization of a million Londoners from the capital. Undermining the planner's dream of a smooth dispersal from the capital was the mass exodus of Londoners who made their own private, individual arrangements for a new life. During the 1950s around 200,000 people – more than were involved in state-sponsored schemes – moved out to swell the population of the Home Counties.

To Abercrombie and the first generation of post-war planners and politicians, this wave of individuals moving out was unimaginable, and they were totally unprepared for it. The great wave of planning legislation passed shortly after the war had appeared to make London safe from this kind of development. It was believed that the Distribution of Industry Act of 1945 which restricted any expansion of industry in the capital and encouraged it to move elsewhere, would disperse many people and jobs to other parts of Britain. And to make sure that London grew no more, the new legislation had constructed a 'green belt' of parks and open spaces within a five- to ten-mile radius of the capital. Conceived as a 'lung for Londoners', there was to be no industrial or housing development inside this area.

However, three powerful forces were driving a hole in these plans and arrangements. First, people in jobs remained in London to a degree none of the experts predicted. No one foresaw that there was to be a big employment boom in offices in London after the war, which was not subject to industrial location control. Many of these well-paid office workers looked for new and better housing, and more and more set their sights on a semi-rural dream home further away from London. Thus pressure on housing in the capital was made even more intense. Secondly, private home-ownership reasserted itself. This was much more difficult for planners to control than the big public housing schemes which the Labour Party promoted immediately after the war. The Conservatives ended restrictions on private house-building and in the affluent 1950s the ideal of home-ownership replaced the socialist dream of mass-housing planned for the public good, provided by a benevolent state. The final factor, which was to shatter Abercrombie's grand plan for London, was the rapid improvement in transport which enabled people to commute to London from further away than ever before. What happened as a result of all this was that new housing developments leapfrogged the Green Belt, and Londoners began to colonize villages and market towns in the Home Counties on an unprecedented scale.

This metropolitan invasion was to transform the character of hundreds of villages in and beyond the Green Belt within commuting distance, either of the capital or market towns like Reading where some of London's offices and industries were beginning to migrate. Farm mechanization and the drift from the land meant that many villages in the Home Counties were experiencing depopulation and were ripe for new development. Middle-class families colonized them in droves from the early 1950s onwards, either restoring run-down cottages or moving into spacious new detached homes usually built on the outskirts of villages. This colonization had begun during the inter-war years, especially in Surrey, but it now advanced rapidly, as faster electrified railway services enabled commuters to travel longer distances more quickly. The electrification of Eastern Region lines to Liverpool Street opened up many Essex villages to London commuters in the late 50s.

An Edwardian view of the village of West Horsley, Surrey, in the days when its economy revolved around the land. This was one of many hundreds of Home Counties villages that were to be invaded by London commuters and transformed into metropolitan villages from the 50s onwards

Much more important, however, was the coming of mass car-ownership. The number of private cars quadrupled in the London area between 1945 and 1960. They were faster and more reliable than ever before and there was a corresponding improvement in the road system. Many used their new car to travel direct to work in London. Frederick Keeble commuted to his office in St James's Square from the picturesque Surrey village of West Horsley, where he and his family moved in 1955:

> I loved driving anyway and thirty miles each way a day wasn't too much for me – it only took about an hour. The only time that it was really tiresome was in the early days when we used to suffer from smog. On one occasion I was coming back and the fog was so thick at Raynes Park that everything was stationary for about an hour and a half, and passengers were wandering in front of cars with white handkerchiefs to lead them home. But usually it was very easy and when I came home in the evening the children, particularly in the summer, were always out on the grass in the drive with their toy tractors waiting to greet me and saying 'How's everything gone?' and they wanted me to take them out for a drive in the car.

Others became car-train commuters. They would drive from the village to the station, park the car, and travel by train to London. In many cases the wife would drive the husband and pick him up in the evening, and queues of housewives waiting for the 6.20 from Waterloo, Victoria or Liverpool Street became a familiar sight in station car parks throughout the Home Counties.

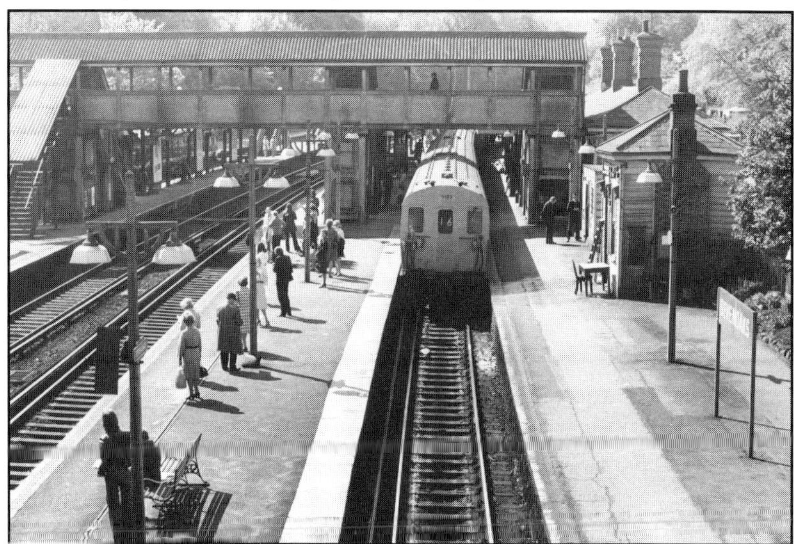

Sevenoaks Station, Kent, pictured in 1966. The post-war years saw a massive growth in car–train commuting. This opened up many villages, which were close to market towns and which enjoyed good rail links to London, to colonization by people working in the capital

Once remote villages that were within striking distance of a station which offered fast trains to London were quickly transformed into booming metropolitan villages by the new car-train commuters. One example of this type of village is Danbury in Essex, situated six miles from Chelmsford, which in turn is only thirty minutes away from Liverpool Street by train. A great monument to the car-train commuter that emerged in Danbury was the double garage. Practically all the new houses which sprouted up in the village from the late 1950s onwards were custom-built detached homes, offering a double garage for two-car families. It was assumed that the husband would drive to the station while the wife would need her own car to get around the village, do the shopping and take the children to and from school.

There were a number of attractions that lured Londoners out to settle in the villages. Many of the post-war pioneers were young middle-class couples born and bred in the suburbs, which were now nowhere near as appealing as they had been to their parents' generation. They were becoming more and more built up, congested with traffic and less rural in atmosphere. There was a strong desire to escape further into the countryside to enjoy the peace and tranquillity that the suburbs were rapidly losing. Village life seemed particularly idyllic to couples with small children and those about to start families like Valerie Keeble:

> The thing that most appealed to us about village life was getting away from the crowds and the noise and the congestion of London. We liked the idea of there being fields and farmland around. And, most important, we wanted the children to enjoy the country life. We wanted them to have space to run around without coming up to a fence, and to throw a ball and not find it in next door's garden. The garden was a great excitement for the children – watching boughs of trees coming down and helping stack logs, and gathering fruits in summertime, helping father pack it away for the winter. And when we got mechanized garden equipment, of course, they had a whale of a time. They were able to sit on my husband's lap and ride on a tractor and trailer when we cut the grass in the orchard, and they had great fun hay-making and watching things grow. And because they had lots and lots of space they were able to have a tent and camp out at night if they wanted to. We bought them miniature tractors and they learnt to ride bikes without having to go out on a main road, which was lovely.

Another magnet drawing Londoners into the countryside was a

growing interest in the architecture and beauty of the traditional English village. Suburbia, with its rows of identical houses, was increasingly seen as boring and artificial. More and more people wanted somewhere more individual and were excited by the idea of restoring an authentic period home in the country, with a real history. Valerie Keeble recalls:

> We'd seen a lot of houses and they were mostly sort of pseudo-stockbroker-Tudor, which we didn't want. We both had a feeling that your surroundings are very important and you can be happy or unhappy in them, according to what they are, and so we'd set our hearts on a period house. We felt there was a certain sameness about a suburban street but in a village like Horsley there was a big mix with period houses, turn-of-the-century artisans' houses, and we liked the mix and the people that that necessarily brought you into contact with, and the variety and the un-alikeness of the streets and the higgledy-piggledyness of it. So we'd seen a house advertised and we had an appointment one November night. We walked up the path and, snap, we both said, 'Yes, this is it' without even seeing the inside. We made an offer there and then, and when I read the surveyor's report I was rather horrified but my husband, who'd got much better professional knowledge about building than me, said, 'No, that's fine', and so we went ahead. It was £4500 which people wouldn't believe today. It was so right with its absolutely genuine façade (the Georgian frontage which so many people try to copy these days without studying proportions) and

Three photographs from the family album of the Keebles, who moved out to West Horsley, Surrey in 1955

Above: Son Simon playing in the back garden

Above right: The Georgian frontage of the Keebles' home as it was when they bought it. Daughter Sarah (right) enjoying riding, a popular recreation amongst the new villagers

> it somehow had an intangible atmosphere and we were just happy in it immediately. It needed some work done on it, but we knew that it was just right.

Most of the newcomers were only dimly aware of the sacrifices and inconveniences of village life. If they had thought more about the possible disadvantages some might have had second thoughts about moving. Most villages were poorly served by main services like gas, electricity and sewers. Improvements took years and often proved very costly. Many village homes, both new and old, had to make do with a smelly cesspit in the back garden. Schools were often few and far between, and some became hopelessly overcrowded as the village population boomed. The new villagers had a similar battle for facilities as their new town counterparts.

But what was most hurtful to many newcomers was the fact that they were often viewed with suspicion and even shunned by the locals. Many middle-class people who moved out shared the romantic ideal that they would be joining a friendly community of rustic villagers. However, the harsh reality was that the locals often resented this colonization by people who were much better off than themselves and who were turning their village into a 'gin-and-jag belt'. They saw their local pubs changing in character; they saw familiar landmarks disappear as their villages doubled or trebled in size; and most important of all they saw the crumbling of the old closed community in which everyone knew everyone else's business. It was this loss of community which accompanied the transformation of agricultural villages, where most people lived and worked locally, to metropolitan villages, where most people worked in London, which was most upsetting to the old villagers. Dorothy Harris remembers how London commuters changed West Horsley in the 1950s:

> In the old days we had horse ploughs and there would be perhaps two men who looked after the horses, and there would be several men out working on the hedges while lots worked on the land. Well, there's still the same roads and lanes now, but much more has been put on them and lots more people live here. Up at the corner, where all the houses are, that was just one orchard belonging to the man across the road, and the kids used to go scrumping apples and pears there. Well, it changed because so many more people came to live here, and they were all such a busy kind. I mean, if they work in London they're out of the village all day so you don't really get to know them. In the old days you used to see men cycling to go up to work down the

> farm, but when the commuters came in they just buzzed along in a car. The car absolutely ruined it: you didn't get to know people like we used to. We would say, 'Oh, that's Mrs Johnson, that's Mrs Childs and that's Mrs Hutchins.' But that's stopped now and you don't get the old friendliness.

While the better off usually settled in and around villages, their less affluent middle-class brethren often colonized more easily accessible market towns twenty to thirty miles away from London, where house prices were slightly cheaper. As a result, places like Guildford, Maidenhead, Bishop's Stortford and Woking became commuter outposts. The key attractions which drew Londoners there were similar to those which were luring them to the villages: car-ownership, faster train services, and a desire to escape from the congested capital.

Although the conventional image of the London commuter is the wealthy stockbroker or the successful executive, during the 1950s even those with low incomes began to commute long distances by rail to work in the capital. This new breed of season-ticket holders were often clerks, foremen or skilled workers, and overwhelmingly they settled in South Essex. The electrification of the line from Liverpool Street to Shenfield in 1949, and then to Southend in 1956 made it convenient to commute from the belt of small towns north of the Thames. A bonus of commuting from here was cheap house prices. In the eyes of middle-class home-owners, South Essex did not have the charm or beauty of the other Home Counties, and few wanted to live there. But the affluence of the time meant that more and more working-class people could afford to buy their own homes, and builders with an eye for this market put up cheap private estates all over South Essex. As a result, towns like Billericay, Brentwood and Rayleigh quickly doubled in size, and between a third to a half of their working populations commuted to the capital. By the late 1950s there were proportionately more people commuting to London from South Essex than anywhere else in the Home Counties.

Abercrombie's plan had assumed there would be a roughly static population but the birthrate rose dramatically in the 1960s and industry continued to migrate into the South East, not only from London but from all over Britain. By the early 1960s residents and councils throughout the Home Counties were up in arms about the invasion of their territory. Although some areas welcomed the jobs and prosperity that the newcomers brought with them, most resented the traffic jams, the damage done to the character of historic towns and villages, and the loss of treasured local countryside under a tide of bricks and mortar. Also there was anger that as offices and factories moved out of the congested capital they dragged semi-rural areas into London's outer metropolitan sprawl. For these were the Shire Counties that London was expanding into, which were overwhelmingly middle class in composition and conservative in their outlook and politics. They wanted to stop or at least regain control over this metropolitan invasion. They were joined in this crusade by many of the newcomers from London who saw the countryside and tranquillity that they had moved out to enjoy threatened by further development. Fears were greatly heightened by planners' projections which suggested that population and industry in the South East would continue to boom in the decades to come.

Clearly a new scheme was needed to replace Abercrombie's plan, which now lay in ruins, if this expansion was to be controlled or contained. One major planning strategy, the South East Study of 1964, claimed that the population of the area would increase by over 3 million in the next twenty years. To accommodate this expansion it recommended an end to piece-meal development and the building of major new self-contained cities at Bletchley, Newbury and South Hampshire, near Southampton, and big new expansions at Aylesbury, Chelmsford, Reading and Stansted (which was also to house London's third airport). This plan never got off the drawing board, but it influenced the new Labour government who were committed to grand planning, and between 1967 and 1968 they designated a second generation of London new towns at Milton Keynes, Peterborough and Northampton. Although similar in some respects to the first new towns, there were also major differences which reflected the fundamental social changes which had occurred since the late 1940s. The second generation were built around fifty to sixty miles away from London, much further out than the first new towns, for there was little space for major expansion any closer to the capital. They were much larger in size and scale than before; Milton Keynes, for example, had a projected population of 250,000. These towns were built with the motor car in mind, and practically every home had a garage provided (unlike the first new towns where garages had to be shared and some roads were too narrow to accommodate parked cars and busy traffic). Finally, they placed much greater emphasis on private building and home-ownership, again in contrast to 1950s new towns, with their near monopoly of state-owned housing.

The showcase new town of the late 1960s was Milton Keynes. It was conceived at a time of affluence and great optimism. But the over confidence of the planners was to have mixed results for those who moved out from London to live there. It was designed like a mini Los Angeles, and was modelled on the assumption that its inhabitants would enjoy an income and life-style similar to that in Southern California, one of the richest areas in the world. The public money that was lavished on it brought an array of advantages for its new inhabitants: expertly designed modern homes, well-equipped schools, every conceivable community facility and, to retain the semi-rural atmosphere of the area, millions of trees were planted and open spaces were beautifully landscaped.

Milton Keynes' road grid system enabled people to drive to work at an average speed of fifty miles an hour, even during rush hours; there were no traffic jams; and there were always plenty of free parking places. Congestion-free roads were made possible by devising a very low-density layout in which industry and housing were scattered over large areas. This seemed to make good sense in the late 1960s when it was assumed that universal car-ownership was just around the corner and that there would be plenty of public money to subsidize buses. But very quickly it became clear that most people couldn't afford to run their own cars. And because the scattered nature of the city made bus services impossible to operate profitably, those who didn't drive often experienced isolation and inconvenience. They had great difficulty in getting to work or to the shops, and some old people and young mothers became stranded. Ironically, although one of the top priorities in the planning of Milton Keynes was to achieve an efficient traffic system, lack of transport was to be one of its most serious social problems. Overall, nevertheless, this space-age city, like the first generation of new towns, provided a far superior environment to the one that Londoners were moving away from.

Despite a few central government projects, like the building of the second-generation new towns, it was in fact the Home Counties themselves which helped determine the fate of people wanting to move out of London. The period from the 1960s onwards was an era when county councils were to wield immense power. Although the Town and Country planning legislation which was passed after the war gave governments the right to purchase land compulsorily for new town developments, at the same time it gave county councils wide-ranging powers to resist any other form of urban encroachment. The noble aim was to prevent ugly suburban sprawls gobbling up valuable agricultural land or beautiful countryside as had happened during the inter-war years. Now county councils, responding to the fears of local residents, were to use these powers to put a brake on the rapid and uncontrolled

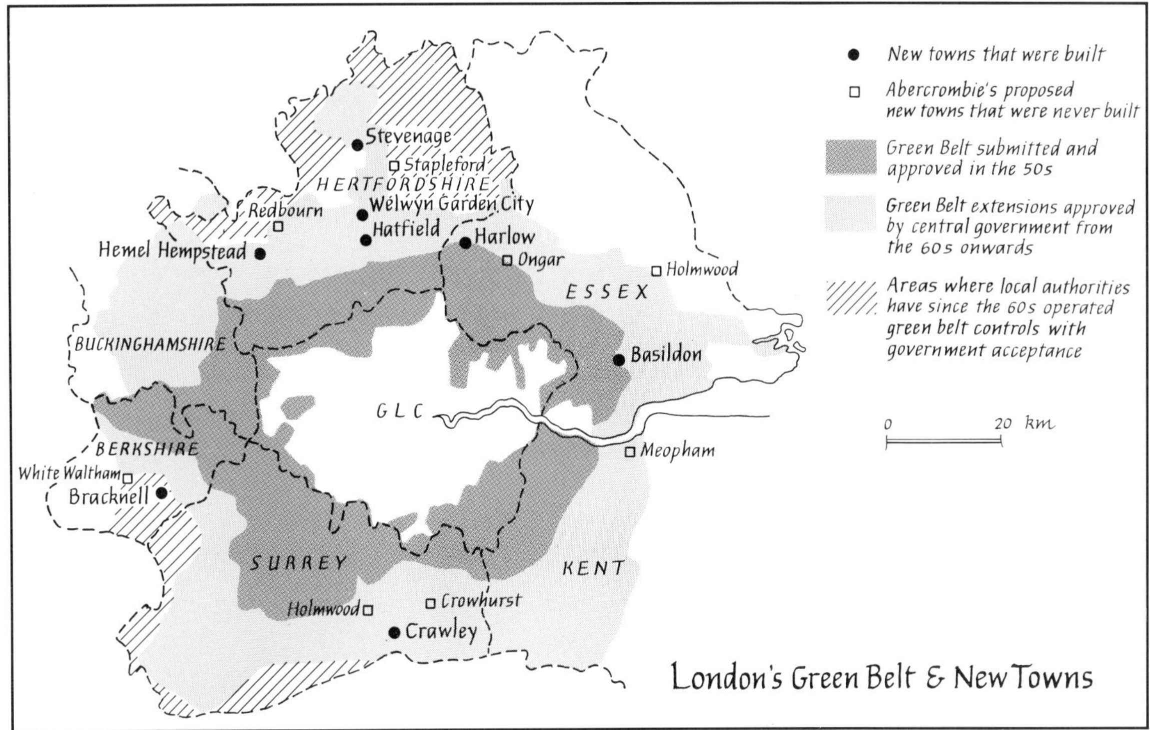

London's Green Belt & New Towns

movement out of London. The main device they used was to extend the land designated as Green Belt. Successive governments were sympathetic to the case put forward by all the Home Counties for Green Belt extensions. As a result, by the late 1960s each of them had doubled, trebled or quadrupled the size of their green belt. Some were quite indiscriminate about what they made Green Belt: unproductive farms, gravel pits, golf courses and waste land were all to be protected against the developer. In the Abercrombie Plan, enshrined in post-war legislation, the Green Belt was on average only about seven miles wide. Now it sometimes extended from between twenty to forty miles. More or less the whole of Surrey and Hertfordshire was designated as Green Belt, and huge chunks of Berkshire and Kent followed suit. These Green Belt extensions undoubtedly did help to contain the growth of London and, in particular, the outer metropolitan sprawl that became marked during the 1950s. But the negative way in which county council powers were used to prevent development was to lead to further problems, especially for Londoners moving out.

In the metropolitan villages the immediate effect of Green Belt restrictions was to send house prices spiralling. Cottages bought in the mid to late 1950s for a few thousand pounds in Surrey villages like West Horsley or Buckinghamshire villages like Chalfont St

In the last twenty-five years house prices have spiralled in Surrey villages like this, partly as a result of Green Belt restrictions

Giles were fetching prices approaching £100,000 twenty years later. Often the concern to preserve the rural character of these villages was genuine, and not primarily influenced by money motives. However, one important consequence of the many campaigns mounted by conservation societies and parish councils to prevent any more building in villages was to add greatly to the market value of the properties in them. Also, the new villagers could continue to enjoy beautiful settings and sometimes spectacular views, all at no cost to themselves. From now on, only the rich would be able to buy their way into these exclusive places, and they would be closed to the vast majority of Londoners.

Conservation policies also, ironically, disadvantaged many of the old villagers by reducing their opportunities for housing, jobs and services. Sky-high property prices meant that from the 1960s onwards sons and daughters of the locals were no longer able to afford to live in the villages where they were born and bred. Many drifted to small council estates built on the outskirts of villages. However, green-belt restrictions and class snobbery kept these council estates to a minimum despite the great shortage of housing for rent in the countryside. And most industrial developments around villages were opposed for environmental and conservation reasons. This resulted in depressed labour markets in and around metropolitan villages which pushed younger people away to find work. One spin-off from this was that middle-class newcomers were able to employ older locals as cleaners and gardeners at fairly low rates of pay. Appropriately, they were often former domestic servants or agricultural labourers who had once worked for the landed gentry. Those who looked to the new metropolitan 'aristocracy' for their employment found a new brand of paternalism, often friendlier and less fierce than the old. Dorothy Harris worked as a cleaner for the Keeble family in West Horsley:

> I'd been in service when I was a girl and I used to have to get up about half past five in the morning, do the fireplace and help the cook. But with Mrs Keeble it was different. I'd just lost my husband and Mrs Keeble was looking for someone to help in her home. When I went round there my mother saw me going off in a sunsuit. She said, 'You're never going round there in a sunsuit to get a job, are you?' I said, 'If she doesn't like it she knows what she can do.' I went for two weeks on approval and stayed twenty years. At first her attitude was rather inclined to be 'well, I'm going to employ you'. But when you got to know her she was sweet. She was a perfectionist in everything she did and you had to do things properly. You didn't say, 'Oh well, I'll do that tomorrow.' But I liked it because we became great friends, we'd sweep the chimney together and do things like that, and I really loved going around there. I went there more for pleasure than for anything else.

As the composition of many villages changed so the services geared towards the old inhabitants were replaced by services directed at the new middle-class community. Village butchers and bakers often became delicatessens or antique shops; bus services were axed because the newcomers often had two cars; and pubs and clubs were taken over by the more educated and well-to-do commuters. Thus, in the process of capturing these village for themselves, the metropolitan middle classes inadvertently helped to destroy one of the things that attracted them in the first place – the original village community. For, despite the new paternalism and devoted work of the newcomers restoring old cottages, the old villagers were in a sense dispossessed by the middle-class invasion.

The extension of the Green Belt was also to have a big impact on market towns and, particularly, on Londoners moving out to them. More land was released for housing and industry in these urban areas than in the countryside, but there was still a serious shortage of land for development. As a result, land prices escalated rapidly which, in turn, pushed up property prices.

Homes on the new private estates built in places like Woking and Chelmsford were often attractively designed with mock-Georgian or classical exteriors, and enjoyed all modern conveniences, like central heating and luxury fitted kitchens. However, because there was so little land available and because land prices were so high, these modern homes were also very small and had tiny gardens. The average size of a semi-detached or detached private home of the 1960s and 70s was far smaller than in the inter-war years. The aim of architects and builders was to pack as many houses into as small a space as possible. Whereas in the 1930s the typical suburban housing density was eight per acre, by the late 60s this had risen to thirteen per acre. These new houses were also smaller than the council- or new town corporation-built homes in the 50s. There were government regulations on minimum space standards, but they only applied to public housing – private builders could ignore them with impunity. The box-like estates that they built, where each house stood cheek by jowl with the next, were to become common sights, especially on the outskirts of market towns, from the late 60s onwards.

The smallness of the new houses created problems for some families moving into them. Although they were often ideal for childless couples, those with two or more children found them very cramped. There was a lack of storage space for items like prams and pushchairs; the kitchens were too tiny to prepare family meals easily; and there was no room in the garden to build an extension to provide extra room. The biggest complaint was the lack of play space for children inside the house or in the back garden. Mike and Rita Brunwin and their two daughters moved out from Cheam into a three-bedroomed detached home on the Goldsworth Park Estate in Woking in 1973. Rita Brunwin recalls:

> The home was smaller than what we'd been used to and that did have some advantages. It was very easy to keep warm and maintain for one thing. But one inconvenience was the small

The Goldsworth Park Estate in Woking, Surrey, the largest private estate in Europe. Because of the high cost of land in the Home Counties, some of the modern homes on estates like this were smaller than the council- or corporation-built homes of the 50s

garden, what with having two children and a big dog. We never wanted our children to play outside in the road – we didn't want them to be a nuisance to the neighbours – but with there not really being the space in the garden it did happen. And because of the traffic we didn't think this was terribly good. It wasn't a safe place for children to be.

Another problem created by land shortages and by the defensive attitude of county councils towards the metropolitan expansion into market towns was the appalling traffic congestion. Councils had no long-term master plan for development, and land that was released for housing and industry was usually made available in a fairly piecemeal fashion. As a result, home and workplace were often separated, for there was little or no co-ordination between housing and industrial developments. This undermined the post-war planner's dream of self-contained communities, modelled on the new towns, in which people enjoyed more leisure time because they lived and worked in the same area. The unhappy consequence was that from the late 1960s onwards the growing army of commuters who travelled to work by car caused traffic snarl-ups, noise, pollution and parking problems in practically every market town on the outskirts of London. During the rush hours, boom towns like Reading and Woking ground to a standstill, and commuters often took half an hour to an hour to travel just a few miles. Local planners tried to keep the traffic moving by introducing by-passes, one-way systems and fly-overs but they sometimes had the effect of ripping the heart out of beautiful market towns and turning them into ugly sprawls. Mike Brunwin remembers his first impression of Woking in 1973:

The first weekend after we moved, I said to Rita, 'I'll pop down into the town and get some newspapers.' And I drove around and came back an hour later and said 'I can't find it.' I drove round and round in circles and it was always just over there. You were stuck in this sort of great big concrete block surrounded by roads, and the result was that you couldn't actually find the town; it didn't basically exist – there was no village street or town high street. So that was, I suppose, one of the biggest shocks that we had when we first arrived, and that took a little time to get used to. But the disadvantages started to come when we found the build-up of traffic getting worse. To begin with, if you decided to drive to London and got away by about seven o'clock you could have a virtually trouble-free run into London and you could make Wimbledon in about

Right: The unplanned growth of market towns in the Home Counties often resulted in serious traffic problems

Above: London's Green Belt has become honeycombed with golf courses. Although it was originally conceived as a 'lung' for city dwellers, the Green Belt has been used to a much greater extent by those who live in the Home Counties

half an hour, but after a time if you arrived on the A3 or the M3 at seven, you hit the height of the rush hour. What was happening was people were starting earlier and earlier as the build-up of traffic got worse and more and more people moved out.

Despite these disadvantages, most of those who left London to live on new estates in the market towns have, on balance, been happy with the move. Factories and offices have continued to colonize the market towns, creating good employment opportunities and reducing the need for long-distance commuting to London for work. Reading, for example, has become one of the fastest growth areas in the country attracting, amongst other companies, Metal Box's head office and Courage's Brewery from London. Constantly increasing house prices, which have partly resulted from the tension between the pressure for development and the shortage of land, has meant that home-ownership in the South East has been a very profitable business. The Brunwins' home in Woking bought for £18,000 in 1973 is in 1986 worth more than £70,000. Property prices for private-estate homes in Woking, and other Home Counties market towns, are amongst the highest in Britain, and everyone who has moved out has shared in this prosperity. Also the Green Belt restrictions have ensured a great wealth of recreational facilities for those living in the Home Countries. There are proportionately more golf courses here than anywhere else in Britain, a host of parks and pretty villages for weekend trips, and many opportunities for country pursuits like horse-riding. Ironically, although the Green Belt was originally conceived so that the city dwellers could enjoy fresh air and country walks, in practice it has been used to a much greater extent by those who live there.

So the vast majority of those who moved out from London in the massive post-war exodus benefited from the move, whether they went to new towns, metropolitan villages or private estates in market towns. Although planning and building failures have presented many problems, on the whole these people have found better job opportunities, better housing and a better environment. The real losers have been those who were left behind. The great flaw in post-war planning was the way so many poor people with so few prospects were allowed to become trapped in the capital. Green Belt restrictions pushed property prices up so high that most people on low incomes could not afford to buy a home outside London. The Home Counties were increasingly resistant to accommodating working-class Londoners on over-spill council estates outside the capital. And the new towns siphoned off skilled workers and prosperous industries leaving the rest behind. In recognition of the growing inner-city crisis the GLC in the late 1960s reversed its policy on the new towns. For twenty years London had supported the development of new towns as a solution to its problem of overpopulation, but now it began to oppose them fiercely, accusing them of robbing the capital of its employment and rates income. The government, fearing cities were being drained of their future life blood, wound up the new town development corporations from the mid-1970s onwards. The 60s predictions of huge population growth, on which the second generation of new towns was based, were proved to be greatly exaggerated by the 70s, and it seemed that any further growth in the new towns would be at the expense of cities like London. Under Margaret Thatcher's government the new towns were to be privatized, and their unique features, like the ownership of land and commercial assets by development corporations operating for the public good, dismantled. London's new towns, once the proud pioneers of a new style of living, were absorbed back into the free market urban system that they had aimed to end. But it was grossly unfair to blame them for what had happened to London. For the overwhelming mass of movement out of London was a private affair which by-passed central government planning and the new towns. In fact it was the failure to plan properly and control this movement out which lay at the heart of London's problems. We look at these problems and at the fate of the people who lived in the inner city in Chapter Six.

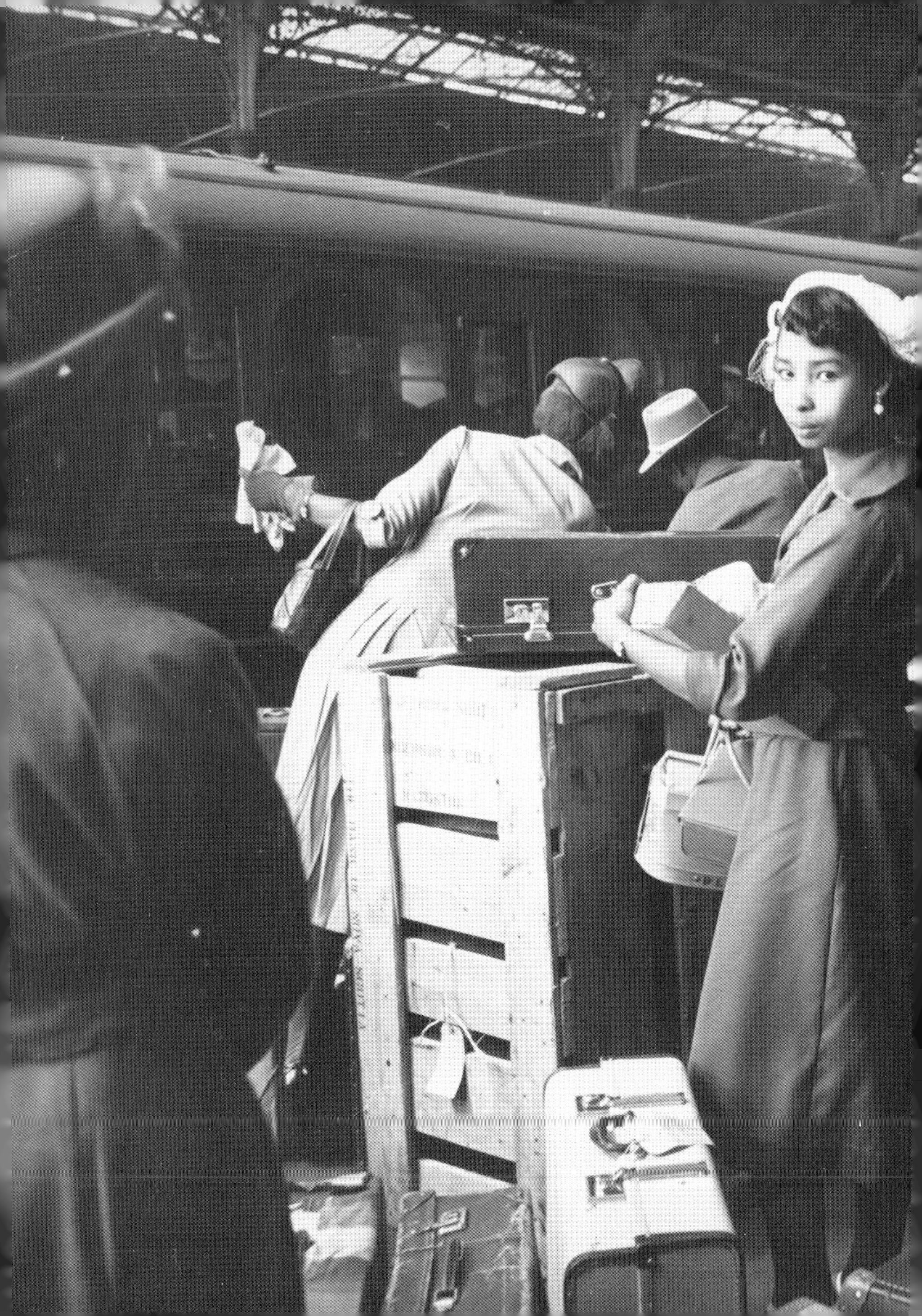
THE BANK OF NOVA SCOTIA

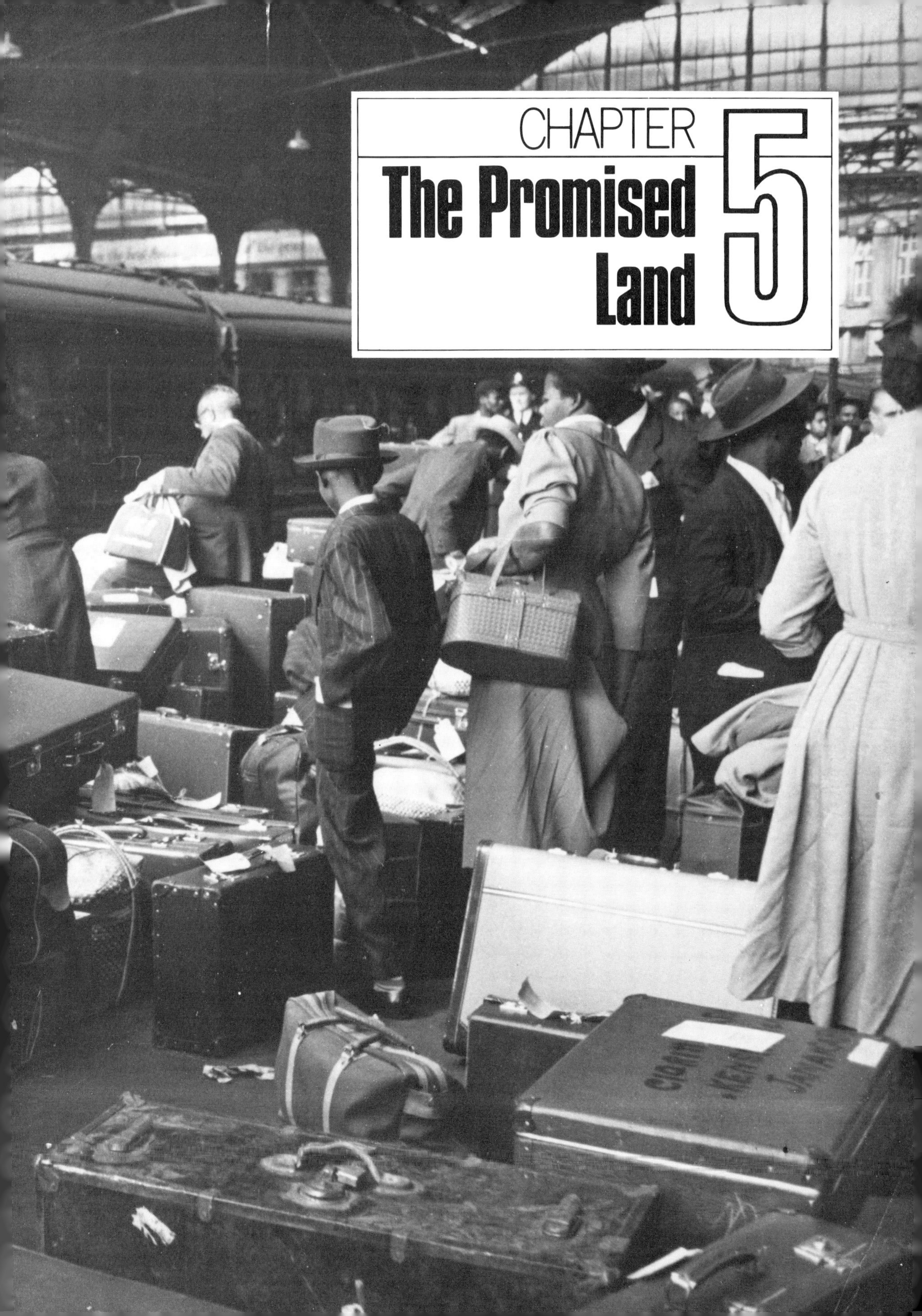

CHAPTER 5
The Promised Land

In June 1948 hundreds of Jamaicans were invited to a civic tea with the Mayor of Brixton and were afterwards introduced to local dignitaries. They had recently arrived on the SS *Empire Windrush* and the account of their coming to the capital was headlined in the *Evening Standard* 'WELCOME HOME'. These were the first black immigrants to come to London from the New Commonwealth in the post-war years. Many of them were ex-servicemen and they came decked out in their 'Sunday best' suits and jaunty hats. Like the later immigrants who followed them they were poor and had to save hard to buy a one-way ticket. Nevertheless, they had high hopes for the future and were determined to begin by making a good impression. London to them was the promised land, a land of much greater opportunity than the one they had come from. The uniquely friendly welcome they received was in part a recognition of the great contribution made by the Commonwealth and Empire to the Allied victory in the Second World War.

Their arrival began a new era in London's post-war history which would transform the capital into a truly multi-ethnic city. Of course, immigration to London was nothing new. Over the centuries it had attracted many poverty-stricken and persecuted peoples. Huguenots from France; Jews from Eastern Europe and Russia; and the Irish. What was distinctive about this latest wave of immigration was the fact that much of it came from the new Commonwealth, drawing in people whose colour and culture was quite different to most Londoners. In the next fifteen years the pioneer Jamaicans on the *Empire Windrush* were to be followed by almost a quarter of a million more immigrants from former colonies and dependencies in the Caribbean, Asia and the Mediterranean. This chapter tells the story of these people who came to London in search of a promised land, and of their children who formed a new generation of non-white Londoners.

Previous pages: West Indian immigrants arrive at Victoria Station in June 1956 after disembarking at Southampton. At this time new settlers from the Caribbean were arriving in London at the rate of 3000 a month

The new Commonwealth was created in 1948 when the British Nationality Act, passed by the Labour government, awarded British citizenship to everyone living in Commonwealth and Empire countries. Their status changed from being imperial subjects to citizens of the Commonwealth with full rights of entry and settlement in Britain. The legislation was inspired partly by our idealism about Britain's role as the mother country, and partly by a practical desire to hold the crumbling Commonwealth together by offering an incentive for membership. Its long-term effect was to encourage mass migration and open the door to these new British citizens.

Migration to London was given a great original stimulus by the upheaval of the Second World War and the long post-war economic boom which followed it. The war had inflicted serious damage on factories, offices, roads, railways, public buildings and housing in the capital. Things had been patched up at the time, but there was much work to be done in the grand reconstruction plan to build a new and better London after the war. Also, war shortages meant that there was a huge pent-up demand for British goods at home and abroad. Thus, following the war, manufacturing industry boomed, fuelling a massive export drive, which in turn created a big demand for labour. However, workers were in short supply after the war. The blitz alone had killed 30,000 London citizens, and many women who had taken waged labour during the war returned home when it finished.

On the other hand, the war had opened up fresh horizons for large numbers of new Commonwealth citizens. Many left their home countries and travelled to different parts of the world to fight. A strong Caribbean contingent volunteered for war service in Britain: for example, 10,000 were recruited into the RAF to work as ground crews. And India provided 2 million men for the Allied forces, some of whom served in Europe. Cities like London seemed to be immensely wealthy and to offer great opportunities to these people. For many of them had been brought up in towns and villages where poverty and high unemployment were endemic – partly as a result of imperial conquest and exploitation. A few set their sights on returning to London to live, while others felt confident and worldly enough to go wherever there was well-paid work after the war.

But very few people from the new Commonwealth would make the passage to London until the early 1950s. For despite awarding British citizenship to everyone in the new Commonwealth, the post-war Labour government actually preferred to recruit European, as opposed to colonial, workers to ease the labour shortage at home. Strenuous and successful efforts were made to recruit European workers, who were seen as more skilled and more suited to the British way of life than their colonial counterparts. There were generous resettlement programmes for East European refugees who did not want to return home to their countries, now controlled by the Soviet Union. For example, around

30,000 Poles who had been in the armed services or who were prisoners of war settled in London with their families after the war. Even the enemies of Britain during the war – thousands of Italians and German ex-prisoners of war – were offered work permits and allowed to stay under the European Voluntary Worker Schemes. All these extra hands were supplemented by a growing wave of Irish immigration much of which was attracted to London. Thus the immediate post-war labour shortage was to a large extent filled by the recruitment of men and women from outside the new Commonwealth.

There was no direct recruitment of new Commonwealth workers in the immediate post-war years, and those who did come paid for the voyage themselves and had no guarantee of work. These disincentives kept colonial immigration to London to a minimum. Just a few hundred West Indians were arriving in the capital each year in the late 1940s, and as late as 1952 the annual figure had only risen to a mere 1500. The vast majority of those leaving the West Indies to find employment abroad went to the United States instead, which enjoyed the twin advantages of higher wages and being much closer to home. The number of Indian and Pakistani immigrants arriving in London was also tiny at this time, numbering less than a quarter of the Caribbean newcomers. The only other Commonwealth country which provided significant numbers of new settlers was Cyprus. Up to the early 1950s around 1000 Cypriots were arriving in London each year.

Most of the early immigrants who did make the journey to London were highly ambitious. More than half of them were skilled manual workers or professionally qualified in some way, and they had high expectations of what could be achieved. Many believed that if they found a good job and worked hard for several years, they would be able to save up enough money to return home to their village or town, set up in business and lead a comfortable life.

For many of the pioneers, life in London in the early days was sweet. Within three weeks all of the 492 Jamaicans who had arrived on the *Empire Windrush* had jobs, most typically as electricians, plumbers, coach builders, labourers and clerical workers. Hundreds of professionally qualified immigrants, particularly Asians, found employment in London as doctors and teachers. Although many had to be content with unskilled and unpleasant work that whites didn't want, they were at least able to find a job of some sort. And the drudgery endured by West Indian street sweepers, Asian factory shift workers and Cypriot kitchen hands, was made less painful by the fact that they were earning

Left: Many early immigrants had to be content with unskilled and unpleasant jobs that white Londoners didn't want. But at least they were able to get jobs of some sort, and their wages were higher than they would have been at home

Above: A Southall house colonized by Sikhs. Most of the early Asian immigrants were men who lived in all-male households

almost double the wage they would have received in a similar job at home.

They also found accommodation without too much difficulty. One of the most important considerations affecting their choice of where to live was the need to be close to their new jobs. Since many of them worked fairly long hours in what by British standards were not particularly well-paid jobs, a time-consuming and expensive journey was out of the question. The areas where immigrants got their first jobs were thus likely to develp as ethnic settlements. In the case of Jamaicans it was to be South-West London, especially Brixton. This was due to the chance fact that Jamaican immigrants in the late 1940s were housed in the old air raid shelters at Clapham, and then directed to South London employment agencies to find work and accommodation. Similarly the Asian settlement in Southall from the early 1950s onwards began because the personnel manager of Woolfe's rubber factory in the town had been a police officer in the Punjab area of India, and he gave many Punjabi immigrants a job there.

Another key factor in the growth of ethnic settlements was the availability of cheap rented accommodation. Brixton initially developed as the main Jamaican settlement in South London because it contained many theatrical and other boarding houses. In what was an old music hall area, where accommodation had been extended to coloured entertainers, there was little of the colour prejudice which sometimes surfaced elsewhere.

Once the settlements were established they began to grow into small ethnic colonies which were to have an enormous impact on the post-war social geography of the capital. Friends and relatives tried to live as close to each other as possible. They provided help in times of need, and their shared ties and shared culture gave them emotional strength in a strange world. However, no real West Indian or Asian community emerged until at least the mid-1950s. The majority of the pioneers were young men who lived to work, saved most of their money and led a spartan existence, often in all-male households. Most did not see London as their real home and they looked forward to going back to their own countries when they had accumulated enough money.

There was, however, an embryonic family-based Cypriot community. During the 1930s several thousand Cypriots had arrived in London, many of them settling in the Camden Town area. Most of them worked in the kitchens of Italian restaurants or in the sweatshops of the Jewish-run garment industry. The war gave them an unexpected boost when as a result of persecution a number of Italians sold their businesses to their Cypriot employees for rock-bottom prices. The new Cypriot restaurants did surprisingly well partly due to the growing popularity of moussaka – a dish made of mince and aubergines – as a cheap and nutritious meal during the war. In the post-war years these new owners recruited friends and relatives from Cyprus to live and work with them in Camden. One Cypriot immigrant was John Nicolas, who came to London in 1947:

> I was sent the invitation to come here by my father's cousin. And my profession was a hairdresser. So he said to me, 'What you like to do?' I say, 'I don't mind, I just want a job.' So we went to a hairdresser and he said to me, 'You're better off not coming to me – go to a restaurant.' So I say, 'I don't mind, I want a job that's all.' So I got a job as a kitchen boy. It was better for me because whatever I got would be clear – I ate there and didn't have to spend my money.

In the mid-1950s, however, the Cypriot community was still very small, as were those of the other immigrant groups. In 1952 the total number of new Commonwealth citizens in London was little more than 10,000 and their tiny colonies had made little impact on life in the capital.

All this was to change between 1952 and 1962, when there was a spectacular increase in new Commonwealth immigration to London. Two key factors pulled immigrants into the capital. The long post-war boom in production continued to create labour shortages. And coupled with greater productivity went greater affluence and a demand for more and better services in the capital.

The Cypriots were particularly well placed to take advantage of this increasing prosperity. With the ending of austerity and rationing, their cafés and restaurants benefited from the revived pleasures of eating out. The Cypriot staff in these establishments had to work very long hours for low pay. But the wages were much better than they could hope to earn back home. On the rare occasions when they returned to their villages in Cyprus, their new wealth was immensely impressive to those they had left behind. This was to encourage many more to emigrate to London. Panayiotis Stavrou Nicolas was amazed at the affluence of his cousin John Nicolas, who returned to Cyprus in 1952 for a holiday after working as a kitchen hand in the capital for five years:

> Every night John and his friends would go to clubs, bars, spending money, and we thought my God, in five years they became millionaires – these boys – so why not us! You know, we had to get to England, but to do that you had to be rich. I asked my father to give me some money to buy a ticket and he didn't have any money obviously. He says to me, 'The only way to do it is to buy a young pig. We feed it for six months, we sell it and then we buy the ticket.' So we did that. Well, it didn't fetch a lot of money and I had to borrow £8 from a cousin of my father as well. Eventually I got to London.

When they arrived, many Cypriots found a new area of London's economy – the clothing industry – was opening up for exploitation. The rag trade had been controlled by Jews since the early part of the century but by the 1950s their success was leading them into other businesses and professions where there was more status and less work. Educated Jewish sons, for example, often became doctors or journalists rather than take over the family business. This created a great opportunity for the Cypriots, who had already begun to colonize the sweated trades working for Jewish employers. Tailoring and dressmaking were important traditional industries in Cyprus and many of the immigrants, both men and women, possessed skills that could be directly applied in London. The sweatshops still used the Victorian technology of the sewing machine and steam press, and what was required to make them profitable was a single-minded work ethic and a determination to succeed.

The Cypriots had both these qualities in abundance, and from the mid-1950s onwards they began to take over London's clothing industry from the Jews. The labour for the Cypriot-owned sweatshops and factories was usually recruited from friends, relatives or villagers back home. As the momentum of the Cypriot economy in

London increased, so too did immigration, rising to several thousand a year by the late 1950s. One of the first Cypriot clothing factories was run by the Nicolas brothers. Tony Nicolas:

> After John had started work in the kitchens, the family had come over bit by bit and by 1953 more or less all of us were in London. Our sister, Nitsa, was working for a firm in Great Titchfield Street, and when she was expecting her first child she had to stop work and her boss gave her a machine to work at home. And that's how our firm started. My other sisters stayed at home to help, then I stayed to help them. John gave up his work as a waiter and we brought another couple of machinists into the basement. We used to sleep there in the evening; we used to sort of push the machines aside and sleep in the same room. In those days we used to work nearly twenty-four hours a day – we put double the time in of anybody else because we were hungry for work. That's why we succeeded – through hard work. And I think within two years we bought a small factory in Chalk Farm Road, we stayed there three years then bought a bigger place off the Caledonian Road, then we bought a factory which was 15,000 square feet off the Holloway Road.

While the Cypriot presence in London was strengthened during the 1950s it was overshadowed by a huge increase in the capital's West Indian population. The average number of West Indian immigrants settling in London between 1955 and 1960 increased dramatically to around 20,000 a year, whereas in 1952 the figure had been less than 1000. London was at this time attracting three-quarters of the total number of Caribbean immigrants to Britain.

There were several reasons for this great influx into the capital. Full employment and increasing prosperity both of which were particularly marked in London resulted in workers having more choice and opportunity. Many Londoners were no longer prepared to undertake dirty jobs involving long hours, low pay and shift work. This problem was made worse by the movement of up to 100,000 people out of the capital each year to live and work. All this meant staff shortages in Central London, and essential services – notably public transport, the hospitals and a whole range of municipal operations – were approaching crisis point. The surplus white European labour force used to solve London's manpower problems after the war was by this stage largely absorbed into the economy, and London now looked to the new Commonwealth for a reserve army of labour.

Some of the new West Indian workers were recruited directly

from their home countries. In April 1956 London Transport began recruiting staff from Barbados, and later turned to Trinidad and Jamaica for more. As an incentive LT paid their fares to London under a long-term loan system, and arranged for accommodation once they arrived. The thousands of eager recruits who were trained to be bus drivers and conductors, or to be ticket inspectors, guards and drivers on the underground, provided the backbone of London's public transport system in years to come. Conservative Health Minister Enoch Powell was involved in the campaign to employ thousands of West Indian women as nurses in the nation's hospitals. And other organizations like the British Hotels and Restaurants Association were also active in recruiting labour in the Caribbean.

However, the great majority of settlers from the new Commonwealth came unaided as voluntary immigrants. One big 'push' factor encouraging Caribbean peoples to come to London was the virtual banning of West Indian immigration to the United States after 1952. Prior to this nine out of ten West Indian migrants embarked for America as opposed to Britain: afterwards these figures were to be reversed and London became the focus of their hopes for a new life. What also added greatly to the lure of London was the whole ethos of 'the Motherland'. Colonial schooling had taught many young people that Britain was the mother country where equal opportunity and freedom were enjoyed, whatever a person's creed or colour. This picture of the motherland was confirmed by many of the settlers in letters written home. They frequently gave rosy accounts of life in London, partly as they were eager to appear successful to those who had stayed behind. When they wrote back to tell friends and relatives of the many job opportunities in the capital those still at home naturally also wanted

A West Indian bus driver and conductor pictured in 1956 at Peckham Garage. London Transport recruited many thousands of workers from the Caribbean – they were to form the backbone of the capital's public transport system

their share of this good life. The reverence for the mother country became so strong, especially in the Caribbean, that some of the migrants coming over actually saw themselves as English men and women. And although Asians and Cypriots did not view Britain as the mother country, they too increasingly saw it as a land of milk and honey.

But the grand dreams of many who made up this new wave of migrants from 1952 onwards were to be broken. Their arrival helped to unleash a rising tide of racial colour prejudice in the capital. Assumptions about the racial superiority of the English over their subject peoples were several centuries old and were closely linked to the development of the slave trade and the Empire. Stereotypes about the inferiority of non-whites remained very strong, for example in popular film and literature, at least till the 1950s. The result was that many Londoners who had never met a black man or woman nevertheless had a rather negative image of what they were like. These engrained imperialistic assumptions had to some extent been laid aside during the war when non-whites made a big contribution to the allied victory. However, by the mid 1950s memories of the war had faded and the old prejudices surfaced again. Added to this, there were fears that what seemed to be an ever-expanding army of poor immigrants would lower wage levels and deprive Londoners of work. And there was a growing feeling that skilled, well-paid work should not be offered to non-whites.

The consequence of all this was increasing job discrimination against non-whites. The blow of racial prejudice was to some extent softened by the fact that a greater proportion of this new wave of immigrants were unskilled and semi-skilled workers from poorer islands like Jamaica. Although they had hoped for something better, many did not complain when they were directed into dirty low-status jobs as street sweepers and factory hands. However, more than a third of the newcomers were skilled or qualified in some way, and it was these that discrimination hurt most. The first taste of this prejudice often came at the employment exchange. Whatever skills West Indians possessed, they would usually be encouraged to enter unskilled jobs. Myrtle Campbell was a qualified teacher who came to London from Jamaica in 1956:

> I went to the Labour Exchange at Balham. And naturally I went to the professional section because I was a professional person and I wanted a good job. That caused a real fuss, they were very embarrassed there. I was told I would be unsuitable, and they sent me to the unqualified, unskilled section. And the jobs they

> offered me there were cleaning and washing jobs that I really didn't want to do.

Applying for jobs direct could be equally frustrating, since some employers and trade unions were reluctant to recruit new Commonwealth immigrants into skilled or white collar jobs. A survey of West Indians in London undertaken in 1958-9 showed that more than half of them had been down-graded as a result of immigration. Myrtle Campbell:

> I applied for a job in the *South London Press*, it was a clerical job for Palmolive and I wrote a letter applying for it. And they wrote back from their head office and actually offered me the job in writing. I had to go to the branch where I was to work and the man from head office would introduce me to the section I was working in. I remember when I arrived at the gate the gateman said more or less, 'What are you doing here?' I produced the letter offering me the job and he eventually let me in muttering under his breath. I sat down but when the section leader came in he took one look at me and ordered somebody to take me straight away from the office entrance where I was sitting, down into the storeroom.

This kind of discrimination was echoed when the new settlers looked for accommodation. The more liberal attitudes which had enjoyed a brief heyday after the war vanished. Signs stating 'NO COLOUREDS' and 'EUROPEANS ONLY' appeared in boarding house windows all over the capital. The same message was spelt out in many 'accommodation available' advertisements in London newspapers. White landlords were often prejudiced themselves or were concerned that housing 'coloureds' might lower the tone of their property in the eyes of other residents, and lead to a fall-off in trade. A study of North Kensington in the late 1950s by Ruth Glass showed that a colour bar was operated even by landlords who did not explicitly state their preferences. She discovered that around one in every six advertisements for accommodation in the local newspaper specified 'no coloureds', but when she rang up the neutral ones 'on behalf of a West Indian friend', only one in every six landlords was actually prepared to offer her a room.

In order to obtain lodgings from a white landlord, immigrants often had to pay high rents and accept squalid conditions. One landlord who dominated this market in North Kensington and who made a fortune out of it was Peter Rachman. He bought around 150 decaying houses in Notting Hill and Paddington, re-

In the late 50s signs stating 'no coloureds' appeared on boarding-house doors and windows all over the capital. One common excuse was that the white residents would not want to use the same bath as a black person

moved the white tenants – sometimes terrorising them with alsatian dogs – and packed in as many West Indian immigrants as possible. These areas became heavily populated with Trinidadians, whom Rachman favoured. Remarkably Rachman was quite popular with his West Indian tenants, despite his corruption and greed, for at least he had provided a roof over their heads when most other landlords turned them away.

The second wave of immigrants were often able to avoid the demoralizing effects of discrimination or extortionate rents through chain migration. Migrants from a particular village or town in, for example, Jamaica or the Punjab or Cyprus, were helped to settle in London by friends and relatives who were already there. Those in London often provided advice, a loan for the fare and help finding a job and accommodation when they first arrived. Migration chains like these have a long history, but they were particularly important in post-war London because of the discrimination and hostility that the newcomers faced.

Another factor enhancing the strength of the immigrant community was home-ownership. By the mid-1950s many of the first wave of settlers had saved up to buy a cheap house in their original areas of settlement in London. They often lived in inner areas like Brixton and Camden that were declining in population and status, and where there was a large stock of old or sub-standard housing

West Indian family life in the London slums in the early 60s. To obtain lodgings from white landlords, immigrants often had to accept overcrowded, squalid conditions and pay high rents

which could be bought very cheaply. These houses were often very large, and although they enjoyed few basic facilities they could accommodate twenty or more newcomers desperate for a temporary home. The availability of cheap and friendly lodgings in West Indian-owned houses quickly turned Brixton into a reception area for Jamaicans coming to London, and its Caribbean population doubled from 5000 to 10,000 between 1955 and 1960.

The presence of growing West Indian settlements in places like Brixton and Notting Hill was by the late 1950s arousing increasing racial prejudice amongst local whites. Wherever they lived they were blamed for lowering the tone of neighbourhoods, bad housing conditions and increased rents. And they met with a frosty reception when they tried to join churches, drink in pubs and clubs or go to dance halls. Sometimes a colour bar resulted in them being turned away. Racist attacks in pubs and streets were becoming daily events, and West Indians began to arm themselves when they went out at night. Lionel Jeffrey:

> To begin with when I came over from Guyana in 1949 things weren't too bad – people were friendlier. But when the masses came over to London there was a lot of bad feeling. You got everything – insults at work, in the street, 'Fucking niggers go home, we'll get you', that sort of thing. There was a fear that

> something violent was about to happen. Sometimes your friends would be beaten up or chased so I started walking around with a hammer in my pocket to defend myself. I always took a hammer with me, I didn't want to use it, but I didn't feel safe without it. And when I rode around on my bike I had an iron bar with me. I'd sellotape it onto the crossbar so that it looked like part of the bike if the police stopped me for carrying an offensive weapon. You would always be asking your friends 'How is it in your area?' to see if there was any trouble. There was always something brewing in Brixton or Stockwell or Ladbroke Grove – the whites were getting very hostile there – and we got very little protection from the police. If things looked bad we'd be phoned up to go over and help out, because if there were a lot of us they'd leave us alone.

This racial tension was to explode into London's first race riot in Notting Hill in late August 1958. For several days and nights the homes of black tenants in the area were besieged by large crowds of whites, some of them several hundred strong, who smashed windows, shouted racial abuse and threw petrol bombs. At the same time gangs of teenagers armed with iron bars, sticks and knives went 'nigger hunting', beating up any blacks they could find. This violence almost triggered off a similar riot in Brixton, but police cordons managed to seal off the area and prevent white mobs from attacking their targets. In the next two weeks an escalation of attacks on black people was reported in Harlesden, Hackney, Stepney, Hornsey and Islington.

Notting Hill riots, August 1958. For several days and nights there were running street fights. The homes of blacks were besieged by large crowds of whites, including many young people

In the wake of these riots there was a Conservative Party campaign for the introduction of immigration controls which received much popular support. The problem of race relations became headline news, and the favoured solution was to reduce or halt the flow of new Commonwealth citizens into Britain. To begin with, the attempt to control immigration was to have precisely the opposite effect to that intended. For while the new legislation was being debated and framed between 1960 and 1962, there was a last great surge of immigration to beat the expected ban. Indian and Pakistani arrivals in Britain swelled from 3000 in 1959 to 48,000 in 1961; West Indian immigration increased from 16,000 in 1959 to almost 50,000 in 1960, then 66,000 in 1961; Cypriot immigration more than quadrupled in 1960 and 1961 when over 25,000 left for Britain; and from all corners of the new Commonwealth, like Hong Kong, immigration reached its highest ever level. Although many South Asians found work in the north of England, the great majority of other immigrants were to live in London. Despite reports of discrimination, London still offered the opportunity of a better standard of living for these peoples than they would have found at home. Chain migration quickly turned the houses of early settlers in Brixton, Southall and Camden Town into virtual reception centres that were bursting at the seams. These pioneer immigrants had been uncertain how long they would stay in London, but the impending legislation panicked them into bringing over friends, relatives and kinsmen from villages so that they would not be stranded and separated from them should they decide to live in London for a long time.

When the Commonwealth Immigration Act came into operation in 1962 this final wave of immigration into London was to be abruptly halted. It brought to an end a brief flowering of liberal, 'open door', policies towards new Commonwealth immigration in the post-war years. From now on only Commonwealth settlers holding employment vouchers would be allowed entry. The numbers and rights of new Commonwealth immigrants were to be further reduced by legislation passed by both Labour and Conservative governments in 1968, 1971 and 1981. In the future, apart from the entry of several thousand East African Asians in the late 60s, much of the new Commonwealth immigration would consist of the relatives and dependants of those already here. The legislation was clearly racist in intent, for it was geared to restricting non-white immigration, while Irish and European immigration continued with no controls.

The rapid shrinking of new Commonwealth immigration which resulted from the legislation was increased by an equally important factor. From 1962 onwards Britain's manufacturing economy entered a period of decline. The never-had-it-so-good years were over, and news of the reduction in opportunities and jobs available in London filtered all over the Commonwealth. If London was no longer eager to welcome labour from the new Commonwealth, neither were those hoping for economic advancement so eager to come.

The early 1960s marked a watershed in the story of their settlement of the capital. The main influx of first generation immigrants born and bred in the colonies was now over. A new era was beginning in which these immigrants would raise their own families, who would emerge as a second generation of British-born Cypriots, West Indians and Asians.

The great liberal hope of the 1950s and early 60s was that new Commonwealth immigrants would be assimilated into the British way of life and would live in harmony alongside white Londoners in the same communities. The actual communities that were formed by the new settlers proved to be very different from this vision. Chain migration, ethnic pride and discrimination by whites meant that colonies from all over the world reformed themselves in different parts of the capital. Particular ethnic groups maintained their identity so that distinct Mediterranean, Caribbean and South Asian settlements appeared. Within these broader racial groupings, communities were formed by people who shared the same nationality, region, religion and language. In some cases colonial villages were more or less transplanted onto the streets of the capital. These ethnic communities brought a new atmosphere and culture to the parts of London where they were formed.

The Cypriot settlement that was established in Camden Town in the 1950s flowered in the next decade into a strong ethnic community known as 'Little Cyprus'. On the surface the Cypriots appeared fairly similar to the host population in their culture, but they were very conscious of what separated them and were keen not to lose their island identity. Although white, they were olive in skin colour; although Christians, they were members of the Eastern Orthodox Church; although some could speak English, they spoke Greek or Turkish as their mother tongue; and although their culture revolved around family life, the family ties that they forged were much stronger and more patriarchal than those which were the norm in London. For all these kinds of reasons the Cypriots formed their own clubs, churches and community centres. Unlike their fellow immigrants from the Caribbean and Asia, their re-creation of colony life was not primarily influenced by hostility from Londoners. Their light skin colour and cultural affinity with the British worked in the Cypriots' favour, and they probably experienced less discrimination than almost any other post-war immigrant group. Their decision to form a distinct Cypriot community in the Camden Town area largely grew out of chain migration and a desire to preserve the culture that they had imported.

Many of the West Indian settlements that emerged in London became outposts of the different Caribbean islands, each with their own identity. Jamaicans were concentrated south of the Thames in Brixton and Stockwell; Trinidadians and Barbadians settled to the west in Notting Hill; the Guyanese colonized north-eastern suburbs like Wood Green and Tottenham; the Montserratians became established in Finsbury Park in North London; and Anguillans based themselves outside London in Slough. The geography of these settlements often originated from the chance factor of where immigrants from particular islands first found work and housing. This was then quickly reinforced by chain migration. The development of these separate colonies was on a deeper level a reflection of the differences in dialect and culture between the islands. The West Indies span 2000 miles of ocean, and until 1960 the only way to fly from Jamaica to Trinidad was via London. The Jamaicans, who spoke an English-based patois, could barely understand the Franco-Spanish dialect of the Grenadians. Many of the islands had different religions. For example, most St Lucians were Catholics, Barbadians were Anglicans and many Guyanese were Hindu or Moslem. And there were important social divisions amongst the blacks themselves; Trinidad had a high proportion of white collar professionals, while Jamaica consisted overwhelmingly of manual labourers. All the unique features of these cultures and the strong rivalries between them were transported into colony life in London. So strong was the separate identity of each island that each had its own clubs and associations, and there were very few mixed pan-Caribbean organizations in London.

The Notting Hill Carnival originated as an expression of the growing pride and self confidence of one of these island communities in the capital – the Trinidadians. It began as an August Bank Holiday event in the early 1960s, with Trinidadian steel bands parading the streets playing the latest calypsos. This was the traditional music of the East Caribbean, and when mothers heard it in the streets many spontaneously stopped their chores and joined the revellers. They were re-enacting the old carnival celebrations that they had enjoyed back home in Trinidad. By 1965 there were dozens of bands and hundreds of dancers, kitted out in home-made ceremonial costumes. From these beginnings the Notting Hill Carnival went on to embrace the growing black pride of West Indians as a whole and become the biggest street festival in Britain.

The South Asian communites that became established in London during the 1960s were, like their Caribbean counterparts, quite separate from each other in culture and identity. One of the largest colonies emerged in Southall, the immigrant boom town of the early 1960s, on which more than 50,000 Sikhs and Hindus were to descend from the Punjab area of India. The dividing line between India and the new state of West Pakistan drawn up by the British government after the Second World War ran right through the Punjab, creating social and political turmoil. Many Sikhs and Hindus who had lived in what was now Moslem West Pakistan fled back to the part of the Punjab which remained in India, but they lost their land and businesses in the process. The poverty and over-population which occurred in the Punjab as a result of this was over the years to fuel the bulk of Indian migration to London.

This Indian colonization of Southall grew out of an earlier settlement of the area in the 1950s by Punjabis. Just as the Jamaicans of Brixton saved up to buy their own homes, so the new Indian settlers clubbed together to take out mortgages on properties in Southall. This was to form the foundation on which the later migration of friends, relatives and kinsmen was based. Southall was also very attractive to the Indians because it was conveniently close to Heathrow airport, which was not only often their first point of arrival but was also a big employer of cheap immigrant labour.

During the 1960s the Sikhs and Hindus began re-creating many Punjabi institutions in Southall. The most important institution which was re-established was that of family life. The pioneer Indian settlers had usually lived in all-male households in order to save as much money as possible before returning home. But when the decision was made to bring over wives and children in the early 1960s, the over-crowded and often squalid male homes practically disappeared. Families bought their own homes, and the money that had once been saved was spent on furnishing and improving them. And the strict, male-dominated family traditions of the Punjab – one feature of which was the arranged marriage of children – were resumed, much to the horror of some liberal Western observers.

Similarly the religious rituals of the Indian sub-continent were reasserted. In the pioneer period few immigrants had observed religious taboos on alcohol and tobacco, and some Sikhs had

Above: Asian newcomers arriving at Heathrow Airport in 1968. Restrictive legislation from 1962 onwards meant that much New Commonwealth immigration after this date consisted of relatives and dependents of those already in Britain

Above left: Muslims in prayer, Regent's Park Mosque in 1978. London's New Commonwealth immigrants often formed their own ethnic communities in the capital which had a quite distinctive culture and religion

stopped wearing their turbans, partly because it made it easier to get a job. However, the 1960s saw a religious revival. Ancient customs were again practised; temples sprouted up everywhere, often in abandoned Christian churches; and male Sikhs proudly began to wear their turbans and grow their hair and beards again, as a striking statement of their religious identity.

What emerged was a tightly knit culture which had few points of contact with the white community that it was colonizing. Many of the immigrants spoke little or no English, and they had little inclination to go to the local clubs, pubs and cinemas. This self-contained life-style actually protected the Indians from much of the everyday white discrimination that West Indians, for example – who shared the language and interests of many Londoners – had to endure.

The most exclusive ethnic community of all to emerge in London during the 1960s, however, was Soho's Chinatown. There had been an original Chinatown, situated not here but in Limehouse in the East End; this small settlement of grocery shops, lodging houses and eating places had since the late nineteenth century provided a base for Chinese merchant seamen and dockers in London, many of whom were originally recruited by the East India Company. The running of Chinese laundries enabled hundreds to move out and set up independently, but the advent of the automatic washing-machine and the launderette in the 1950s put them out of business. However, at the same time greater affluence, a developing taste for foreign cuisine (especially Chinese food), and the growing popularity of eating out provided an attractive alternative for the Chinese in London – the restaurant trade. Many sold their laundries and moved into catering. The Chinese community was transplanted from Limehouse to Soho in the West End, where cheap property was available and which was much better situated to take advantage of the boom in eating out.

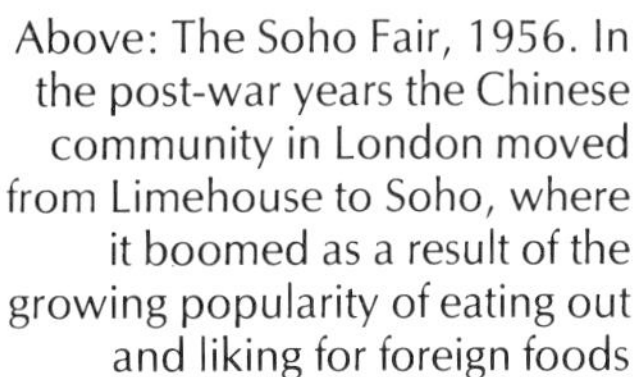

Above: The Soho Fair, 1956. In the post-war years the Chinese community in London moved from Limehouse to Soho, where it boomed as a result of the growing popularity of eating out and liking for foreign foods

Above right: Mr Mann and his wife when he married in Hong Kong in 1962. Like many other Chinese immigrants in London he went home to find a bride, then paid for her to come over and join him

Such was the demand for Chinese food that thousands of villagers from Hong Kong were recruited each year to work as chefs, waiters and kitchen hands in the capital. Many were formerly struggling paddy farmers, who came to London through a process of chain migration to better themselves and provide security for their families. The immigrants rarely spoke more than a few words of English and had no desire to mix with Londoners, whose way of life they found completely alien. By the mid-1960s part of Soho had become an island of Chinese culture, referred to by the newcomers as the Imperial City. But the strongest ties of all remained with the home villages back in Hong Kong. Savings were sent back every month; land or homes were bought with a view to going back eventually; and trips home were made every few years. For most young single men like Mr Mann, the motive behind visiting the home village was the quest for a bride:

> I came over in 1959 to work in restaurant in London. There was much poverty in Hong Kong and I wanted better life. I write to my girlfriend there, she lives close to my village, and we talk about marriage when I come home. I save up to come back in 1962, that was when we get married. Then I come back to London, leave her there, because I didn't have a proper home for her to come to. I was very homesick and lonely leaving her. But in two years I had more money and a home and she come over to join me.

With the rapid growth of all these ethnic communities in London during the 1960s, there was a necessity for each one to

An Indian cinema in Southall, pictured in 1976. Run-down cinemas in areas like this were given a new life under Asian management, showing Indian films to packed audiences

develop an internal economy to service its special needs. The one real exception was the West Indian community, which had no entrepreneurial tradition and which as a result of colonial penetration shared similar tastes to the British. Restaurants serving authentic Cantonese and Indian food – as opposed to the bland dishes prepared for the British – sprouted up in the streets of Soho and Southall. Butchers, grocers and clothes shops selling traditional foods and costumes mushroomed in all the ethnic quarters. Ethnic estate agents and banks became very popular, partly because they seemed to offer a certain way of avoiding discrimination. Also, the entertainment needs of each community were provided for. Run-down cinemas were given a new life when under Asian management they began showing Indian films to packed audiences. And gambling clubs, ever popular with Chinese workers, sprang up all over Soho. Gerrard Street in Soho came to be called 'the Chinese Peoples' Street', because it provided a great array of Cantonese eating places, grocers, book shops, travel agencies, and so on, making it a regular place of pilgrimage for the Chinese from all over Britain.

The flowering of ethnic communities all over London in the 1960s met with an intolerant response, however, the effect of which was to damage race relations even more. The decade was to see the rise of a fierce racial hostility against non-whites, and the emergence of race as a major social problem. The troubles were usually concentrated in the areas which had been most heavily colonized by immigrants. White residents associations, for example in Southall, compaigned to prevent any more immigrants from buying houses and moving into their areas, and put pressure on the local authorities to send black children to separate schools.

There were dozens of unofficial strikes and walkouts staged by white Londoners who refused to work alongside blacks. Street violence against non-whites also became a regular occurrence in the capital. The most turbulent area was Spitalfields, where a large Bengali community, recently arrived from East Pakistan, was eking out a living from long hours of toil in sweatshops. The local whites objected to their presence, and from the old East End streets emerged the skinhead sub-culture – later to be copied on a nationwide basis.

One of the main interests of these working-class teenagers with their distinctive uniform of bovver boots and cropped haircuts was 'Paki-bashing'. By the late 1960s attacks on Pakistanis with bottles, boots and knives had become a regular pastime in the East End, especially in the Brick Lane area. This was the decade when Enoch Powell rose to prominence with his rabble-rousing speeches advocating the end of immigration and a policy of repatriation. The London dockers and Smithfield porters were to down tools and march to the House of Commons in his support. In 1968, the same year that Powell was making his most rabid speeches, the Labour government passed a new Race Relations Act offering protection to non-whites against discrimination in employment, housing and services. This legislation is sometimes taken as a sign of a new liberalism on race. However, the very fact that the legislation was necessary is powerful evidence of the growing crisis in race relations at this time.

A number of anxieties lay behind this rising tide of racism. The 1960s were a decade when the Commonwealth was in rapid decline, and it was very difficult for a nation brought up to believe it was a superior race to accept former imperial subjects as social equals and near neighbours. Also closely knit white communities in inner London were gradually disintegrating and the immigrants' presence was a convenient scapegoat for a social charge that was, in fact, caused by grand planning, housing redevelopment and unemployment (see Chapter Six). There was a growing fear, especially in areas where there was a large ethnic population, of being swamped by an alien culture.

Yet, while the concentration of ethnic colonies in various parts of London during the 1960s gave some substance to these fears, in fact a reverse process was taking place at the same time. A minority of immigrants with sufficient capital and confidence were moving out to predominantly white suburban areas either to live or to work. They took with them Victorian values like the work ethic, and gave new life to Victorian institutions that were under attack from the individualism and consumerism of swinging London. This was one of the great ironies of the debate about the threat that immigrants posed to the national way of life: the colonial influence on their culture meant that they were often more strongly attached to traditional values than the British.

The corner shop is one traditional, taken-for-granted institution which would certainly have become a rare sight in the London suburbs had it not been for the entry of Asians into the retail trade. By the mid- to late 1960s corner shops in the London suburbs seemed doomed in the face of competition from the cheaper supermarkets where practically everything could be bought under one roof. Many went to the wall or tottered on the verge of extinction. It was from this time onwards that newsagents, grocers, off-licences and chemists were bought up at rock bottom prices, often by Sikhs and East African Asians. In many cases the new owners made them profitable by opening all hours, seven days a week, and by using cheap family labour. They were to become immensely important for the old, the poor and housewives without cars in the capital, who needed shops that were conveniently close to where they lived.

Another area of retailing in which immigrants applied Victorian values of hard work, thrift and family independence with great success was the restaurant business. From the mid-1960s onwards there was a mushrooming of new and exotic restaurants serving foreign foods in almost every high street in the capital. Thousands of Indian, Chinese and Greek family restaurant businesses followed the earlier example of Italian spaghetti houses, and cashed in on the increasingly cosmopolitan tastes of Londoners. The opportunity that these restaurants offered to sample the food, music and atmosphere of different cultures was warmly welcomed by

An Asian-run general grocery store in the capital. Asians took over many corner shops from the early 60s onwards and made them profitable by opening all hours and using cheap family labour

many Londoners. And in the process, conservative British eating habits were revolutionized. Mr Mann:

> I work as cook in Chinese restaurants for about ten years. Lots of people wanted Chinese food so I save up (it didn't cost a lot to open a take-away), I borrow from a friend and a bank, then I start my business. I open it 1969. I had an advertisement in a local newspaper and I put up very big posters on my shop front saying when it would open. I also print a lot of menus with my name and address on them, then I take these menus round house by house so that people would know about the take-away. It went well the business, the people were very friendly, they liked the food and often they come back for more.

During the 1960s it became clear that the more successful and prosperous new Commonwealth families were moving away from their original colonies to more suburban homes, following a similar path to that trodden by the Jews in previous decades. They were often more devoted to traditional suburban values like pride in home-ownership, church attendance and family respectability, than were the Londoners who were established there. Cypriot families who ran successful clothing or catering businesses often moved north, first to Harringay, then to Enfield, Barnet, Brent and Waltham Forest. The symbols of success like detached homes and expensive cars were very important to them, and as early as 1966 almost half the Cypriot householders in London were owner-occupiers. Another attraction of suburban life for Greek-Cypriots like the Nicolas family was the open spaces which reminded them of the villages that they had migrated from. John Nicolas:

> To start with I lived with my sisters and brother in a house we bought near Regents Park. Then by the early 60s all the family started to move out to Finchley, and the feeling was always to get out, as you did better in life. You wanted to be out in the open, because we came from a village and we liked the open; we missed all the countryside.

In the 1960s there was also a strong outward migration of West Indian families from the central areas to the London suburbs. One particularly popular area was Croydon, where around three-quarters of the several thousand-strong West Indian population were home-owners. This was actually a higher rate of home-ownership than was the norm amongst British-born London families. Most of the West Indian householders in places like Croydon were skilled or semi-skilled manual workers who saved hard to pay their mortgages. Many brought with them a passion for church-going and cricket that harked back to the days of the Empire. Myrtle Campbell remembers:

> It was the ambition of everyone coming over from Jamaica to have their own home. So for years we'd save every penny we could: no holidays, my husband gave up his drink and cigarettes, and he took every minute of overtime he could get, sometimes the children didn't see him from one week to the next. Well, we'd been living in rooms in Clapham and it was difficult with four children because there was no space and we didn't want them playing in the streets with all the traffic. We decided to move to Croydon and when we saw this home we just fell in love with it. It was about £8000 at the time – it was a dream come true. The most important thing for us was that we had a back garden which gave the children so much more freedom to play. We were one of the first West Indian families in our end of the street and people were very friendly. The old woman next door was like a mother to the children and they used to play in her garden. And there was a lovely Roman Catholic church near here. We had the boys baptized there, then they became altar boys and we'd go to mass every Sunday morning. We were

During the 60s there was a strong outward migration of West Indian families from the central areas to the London suburbs. The Campbell family moved from a flat in Clapham to a semi-detached in Croydon in 1964. Left: Roy and Myrtle Campbell at the baptism of their daughter Lorraine. Far left: Daughter Janet and son Michael pictured in the Campbells' front garden. Below: Sons Michael (fourth from left, second row) and Louis (back row, centre) who became altar boys in the local church

church people and we felt that our children should follow us. I suppose because I was a teacher I wanted the children to do well at school so I gave them a lot of tuition at home, reading them books, answering their questions, and it paid off because they all did well and my eldest son won a scholarship to the local grammar school. My husband was very keen on cricket – he played with the boys out in the back garden with a real cricket ball. It was a regular thing to have all the windows smashed. But they did well and Michael and Louis are both good cricketers now.

At the same time as many new Commonwealth immigrants were achieving respectability in the eyes of their suburban neighbours, so their children were also becoming more integrated into the mainstream 'white' culture of London. This mixing was greatest amongst the children of families who were dispersed in the suburbs, but it also occurred in ethnic communities. For this second generation of British-born non-whites went to schools where English was the first language, where 'Western' ideas formed the basis of the curriculum, and where they mixed and made friends with the white London children. This education made them more receptive to the influence of Western books, magazines, radio and television than their parents, some of whom spoke little or no English.

The adoption of some western and individualistic values by young Asians, Cypriots and West Indians was to create a generation gap between themselves and their parents, who were usually strongly committed to the traditional culture. This conflict between the first and second generations of newcomers was heightened by the impact of Western 'pop' culture, which was embraced to some degree by many young people. Disputes with parents over dress, late-night discos and young love affairs often concerned teenage girls who in some cases had marriages arranged for them and were expected to be virgins on betrothal. The patriarchal domination of women in these traditional ethnic cultures contrasted sharply with the freedom and sexuality that were encouraged in the new commercialized world of youth.

In fact, the 'youth' culture that bloomed in London during the 1960s was itself heavily influenced by non-whites, some of whom took advantage of the new careers it offered, especially in the music business. The Afro-Caribbean culture had influenced popular music for many decades and it was particularly important in the 'pop' explosion of the 1960s. Black rhythm and blues and modern jazz became cults among the London Mods; the Ramjam

Club in Brixton, which featured Gino Washington's band, became a seedbed for soul music; Georgie Fame and a number of other trendsetting London singers increasingly employed black musicians in their line-up; and ska and bluebeat were adopted as the music of the skinheads. In all this new music there was a very heavy borrowing of traditional Afro-Caribbean dances which were much more informal and sexual than their British counterparts. Some of the most exciting young dancers featured on the television programme 'Ready Steady Go', for example, were West Indians. They helped to develop a modern style of individual dancing now taken for granted as part of our culture.

By the beginning of the 1970s, then, there were a number of different dimensions to the new Commonwealth experience in London. Important ethnic communities had been established; racial hostility and discrimination was on the increase and was directed particularly at these colonies; yet the more successful non-whites were becoming integrated into suburban life, and the second generation of London-born blacks were growing closer to white youth in the capital. The recession which undermined London's economy from the early 1970s onwards was to have a profound impact on this emerging relationship between new Commonwealth minority groups and the mainstream culture. For it was precisely those areas of the capital's economy in which new Commonwealth workers were most heavily concentrated that bore the brunt of job losses. The rapid decline of manufacturing industry, the sweated trades and public services in London resulted in unemployment amongst new Commonwealth groups rising at around double the rate it was for whites. Some of the old inner city colony areas like Brixton began to turn into ghettos where high unemployment, bad housing and social deprivation were concentrated.

The position was worst for young blacks, many of whom were brought up in poverty and benefited little from an education system that was geared to the needs and interests of white children. Most left school with few qualifications and were then confronted with racial discrimination by employers. Few were able to get jobs, and the unemployment rate amongst West Indian youth in London rose to 40 per cent by the early 1980s. Experience of disadvantage and discrimination had a big influence on the identity of the new generation of London-born blacks, who by the mid-1970s represented about two in every five black people living in the capital.

The greatest impact was on West Indian youth, who formed the most deprived section of London's society. Out of their shared sense of resentment and injustice a new, defiant pride in being black was born. A collective Afro-Caribbean identity began to emerge amongst the younger generation, which transcended the old island loyalties and rivalries. Whereas the older blacks had tried to fit in to white society, some sections of black youth now turned away from it to form a distinct culture of their own. Some adopted Rastafarianism, a religious movement that grew up in the West Indies in the 1930s and looked to Africa as the spiritual homeland. It condemned white society as greedy and corrupt (Babylon), rejected the work ethic and celebrated the smoking of ganja (cannabis) as a way of achieving communion with God. And it was fuelled even more by reggae music, notably that of Bob Marley, who quickly became the high priest of Rastafarianism.

This rebellious sub-culture merged with another tradition of the black colony which became much more important in an age of mass unemployment. This was the tradition of living outside the law through street-wise 'hustling', which usually involved illicit drink, drugs, petty crime and prostitution. One crime particularly favoured by black teenagers which emerged out of this twilight world in the early 1970s was robbing people as they walked home along dark city streets in places like Brixton. The disturbing image of young blacks flouting the law and attacking innocent whites was to unleash another wave of racism upon them in the capital. The media created a moral panic by dubbing these crimes as 'muggings' and grossly exaggerating their extent and the violence associated with them. At the same time the Metropolitan Police swamped black areas with a new style of tough policing which resulted in many unfair arrests and the criminalization of whole communities. This racial antagonism, aggravated by increasing unemployment and the poverty of inner-city areas, was to explode into serious riots of black youth against the police, notably at Brixton in 1981 and at Broadwater Farm, Tottenham, in 1985.

However, it would be misleading to end the story of new Commonwealth immigration with battles on the streets of London. The black youths involved in Rastafarianism, riots and muggings have for the past fifteen years formed only a small minority of the West Indian population in the capital. The majority have remained 'respectable', church-going and hard-working – where there is work to be found – and have a renewed pride in their black identity. And although many young blacks do, with justification, feel disenchanted with the way they have been treated, this resentment does not occur to anything like the same extent amongst the London-born children of most other new Commonwealth groups. This is partly because the Asian, Chinese and Cypriot newcomers established a much stronger economic foothold in the capital, often through the ownership of small businesses. These groups enjoy a higher standard of living and more opportunities than their West Indian counterparts. Also their cultures and communities have been more tightly knit than those from the Caribbean. This has provided a greater sense of security and purpose for the second generation who were born in London, and has insulated them from much discrimination. Despite the fact that conflict between teenagers and parents has been documented, for example amongst London Sikhs and Cypriots, most have reverted to an adaptation of traditional values in their adulthood. Thus for many new Commonwealth groups the journey to London in search of the promised land and a better life for their children was not a wasted one. Indeed, for a minority like the well-to-do Cypriots of Edgware and Hendon, their dream came true, often as a result of relentless hard work and entrepreneurial drive. Even if the majority were disappointed, both with the reception and the rewards they received in London, this was tempered by the fact that they were better off than if they had remained at home. Although racial disadvantage and discrimination in London should not be forgotten, neither should the many achievements of the new settlers and the positive contribution they have made to life in the capital since the war. Many have brought a new spirit of enterprise and commitment to declining inner-city areas. A lot of the services taken for granted by Londoners, like underground trains, buses, hospitals, and corner shops, could not have been kept running had it not been for their willing hands.

CHAPTER 6
Inner-City Dream

In the summer of 1951 millions of Londoners visited the Festival of Britain, a government-sponsored extravaganza of entertainment, on the South Bank between County Hall and Waterloo Bridge. On what had been a patch of wasteland a new generation of architects had built a miniature wonderland, which included the Dome of Discovery, the largest dome ever constructed, and many modern designs, like the Skylon – a silvery aluminium object which appeared to be suspended in mid-air. A great

Previous pages: The eighteen-storey high Brandon Estate in the course of construction in Southwark, 1959. Flats like these were at the heart of the dream for a brave new world for London in the 50s and 60s

The Skylon – one of the futuristic sights to be seen at the Festival of Britain on the South Bank in 1951. The Festival was a showcase for the better world that Londoners had fought for during the war

array of amusements were provided upstream at Battersea in the Festival Pleasure Gardens. And buses ferried visitors to the Exhibition of Living Architecture in the East End. Here, a new neighbourhood called Lansbury was being built to replace the bombed terraces of Poplar. Lansbury was named after George Lansbury, Poplar's famous leader of the Labour Party, and it represented an idealistic vision of the city of the future that Londoners could look forward to. The standards of comfort and convenience in the new council flats and houses at Lansbury were higher than ever before. To most of the Londoners who admired the Lansbury Estate and who strolled around the pavilions on the South Bank exhibiting new homes (complete with television sets) and gardens, the Festival was a showcase of the better world that they had fought for during the war.

This chapter tells the story of the new city that politicians planners and architects tried to build after the war. We focus in particular on the experience of one poor inner-city borough, Islington, to show how for many the dream was to turn into a nightmare.

Islington had not always been poor. Much of it was built in the nineteenth century as a suburban retreat for well-heeled city workers. Canonbury and Barnsbury were quite expensive and exclusive areas where bankers and stockbrokers lived, while Holloway – the home of the fictional Mr Pooter – was peopled by more humble clerks. Islington went into decline from the 1870s onwards as the poor spilled out from the teeming central areas. Its middle-class residents took advantage of improved railway communications to move further out into the country. Their homes

Below: The Lansbury Estate in the East End, part of which was completed for the Festival of Britain. It was built to very high standards and represented the idealistic city of the future

Inset: The first family to move into a flat on the estate, February 1951. The standards of comfort and convenience in the new council flats and homes here were higher than ever before

were sub-divided into cheap tenements for workers. Thus Islington took on a working-class character, with hawkers, sweat shops and home workers colonizing its once elegant Georgian squares and terraces.

The Second World War added greatly to the housing problems of poor areas like Islington. By 1945 huge tracts of inner London had been turned into a bomb-shattered and weed-covered wasteland. The blitz, followed by the doodlebug and rocket attacks on the capital, had devastated its housing stock. In Islington 3000 houses had been totally destroyed by Hitler's bombs. Many thousands more had suffered serious bomb damage to roofs, walls and windows, all of which had been hastily patched up. Islington's plight was not quite as desperate as that of the East End; in Stepney, for example, the blitz had demolished and made uninhabitable a third of the housing. However, the long neglect by the landlords who controlled its tenement slums, combined with lack of repairs and destruction during the war, meant that Islington had some of the poorest housing in the capital. Three-quarters of its households did not even have running water, an inside lavatory nor a bath.

Yet the very destruction of the war inspired politicians and planners to come up with utopian ideas for a new London that would rise out of the ashes. The blueprint of a better world for places like Islington was contained in the plans for London drawn up during the war by Patrick Abercrombie. The aim, as we have seen, was to reduce over-crowding through a controlled dispersal of a million Londoners and their jobs to new towns and estates in the South East. For those who remained he planned new communities which would enjoy a higher standard of housing, facilities and open space than ever before in a public scheme in Britain.

However, a government cash crisis and crippling lack of building workers and building materials in the immediate post-war years meant that Abercrombie's grand plan and the housing drive in London were delayed. It seemed to many Londoners that the promises of a better world which had helped to sustain them through the sacrifices and sufferings of the war had been pie-in-the-sky. Housing conditions had actually deteriorated, for the slum streets which many had lived in before the war were now made worse by bomb damage. In Islington, for example, there were 12,500 families on the council waiting-list, amongst whom were the Cassallis. Ron Cassalli remembers:

> The housing conditions we lived in then [before the war] were atrocious. We had sixteen people using one toilet, three

Left: Jubilee Buildings, Wapping, in 1949. Many inner London families had to put up with Dickensian housing conditions after the war

Above: Squatters take over Abbey Lodge at the end of Hanover Terrace in the West End in September 1946. The wave of squatting which swept across the capital in that year was one expression of the anger and desperation felt by many people at the appalling housing conditions of the time

> families queuing up and there were eight of us, my wife and six children, in two rooms. Then along came the war and the ceiling was damaged and water started seeping in through the cracks in it. We had eight people sleeping in this one bedroom with water seeping through the ceiling, buckets everywhere, and every now and then your bed got wet. And if one of the kids was ill, had a cough or something, it woke the others up. Terrible conditions to live in and to think we'd spent six years of our lives fighting a war, and we had to come back to this kind of thing. I was very annoyed; I felt really let down.

A mood of anger and desperation was in the air. In the summer of 1946 thousands of poor and homeless families took the law into their own hands by squatting in empty buildings and military camps. And in September of that year the Communist Party organized a well-publicized squat by about 1500 East Enders in luxury West End flats which were being renovated. Hundreds of families carrying bedding and pots and pans converged on High Street Kensington and seized Duchess of Bedford House, a seventeen-storey block of flats. They also invaded other Kensington mansion blocks in Upper Phillimore Gardens and Holland Park, and captured the 630-room Ivanhoe Hotel in Bloomsbury. The squats ended after about two weeks when eviction notices were served, but the angry mood continued and was reflected in many individual acts of defiance. In the exceptionally cold winter of 1947, for example, the impoverished Cassallis used desperate measures to get free fuel for their fire:

> Those were very hard days – so hard that when it got cold in the winter and you couldn't get coal we used to go next door (it was an empty house that had been bombed). And, first of all, we took the coal that was there in the coal cellar, then we took up the floorboards, then we used the bannisters – anything that was burnable we would burn. And many a time I remember lying in bed thinking, 'How the hell am I going to pay these bills?' and even contemplating doing burglaries and things like that which I'd never done in my life. Things got so desperate, that's the way you felt.

But by 1948 things were looking up a little. The first improvement felt by many was, however, not in housing but health care. The National Health Service came into force at midnight on 4 July. With the coming of the welfare state, inspired by the Labour Party, people enjoyed new welfare rights. There was an enormous take-up of benefits in poor areas like Islington. Especially welcome was the free medical treatment, and the free spectacles and false teeth which the poorest had been forced to do without in the past.

The creation of a comprehensive system providing health care for all, from cradle to grave, was one of the great planning achievements of post-war years. And on the housing front things were also improving by the late 1940s. Production of the first pre-fabricated houses, quickly dubbed 'pre-fabs', was stepped up, and many thousands of these rabbit hutch-like bungalows sprang up on bomb sites all over London. Although they were seen by the government as a stop-gap measure which would have a short life, they turned out to be one of the few triumphs of pre-fabricated building in the post-war years. Especially popular amongst the residents was the fact that they offered privacy, and a cottage garden in a detached or semi-detached setting. Betty Vodden remembers being shown her new prefab in Islington in 1947:

> In 1947 my husband came out of the Navy and lodgings and houses were so hard to get, we couldn't live together. I went to live with my mother and we were well overcrowded there, and my husband lived twenty minutes' walk away. This lasted for about two years and by then I had a son of eight years and a baby of eighteen months. So one day the woman who took my mother's rent came round and asked me if I'd go with her up the

A proud 'pre-fab' resident in Camberwell tends his prize-winning garden in 1948. 'Pre-fabs' were very popular because they offered modern conveniences, privacy and a cottage garden in a detached or semi-detached setting

> road. When I got to the top of the road she turned the corner and I knew there were eight pre-fabs there and I said to her, 'You're not taking me to a pre-fab?' She said, 'I am.' Oh, when I got there I was so thrilled with the lovely big gardens all waiting to be dug up. We went in through the side door and it opened on to the kitchen. It was beautiful: there was a 'fridge which was something I'd never had before, an electric cooker, electric kettle, lovely tops, wooden tops to everything. Everything was grand and I was really thrilled when she gave me the key, especially as we could live together then.

By 1948 the LCC rehousing programme in Central London was beginning to bear fruit. Looking back at this period, one is struck by the modest scale of the architecture and the sensitivity to social needs which produced a rather old-fashioned look. The LCC insisted on a maximum height of six storeys for the flats it built. These made ideal homes for families like the Cassallis who were moved out from the tenement slums:

> We were given a four-bedroomed LCC flat on the second floor which was absolutely heaven. The four main things we liked, in order of priority, were, firstly, to be able to sit in the toilet on your own, undisturbed, nobody knocking on the door, and to contemplate, and really enjoy yourself. Secondly to have a bathroom; thirdly, to have hot water and fourthly, to have the

Above right: New LCC flats rise out of the Dickensian slums of inner London in the late 40s. Most of the flats built at this time were no higher than six storeys and were a great improvement on the tenement slums that they replaced

Above: A mother and child who moved from their squalid home into an LCC flat enjoy the luxury of a bathroom for the first time

> privacy of your own front door. Nobody could appreciate how marvellous it was unless they'd gone through the drama of having one toilet for sixteen people for all those years.

Even in its grandest project, the Lansbury Estate, the LCC insisted on a rich variety of form. Lansbury was begun in 1948 as part of the Comprehensive Development Scheme for Stepney and Poplar, which aimed to rehouse 100,000 people in the East End in a mixture of modern flats and houses. Community facilities like schools, churches, shops, civic centres and play areas were to be provided in abundance.

Lansbury, however, was not the beginning but the end of the Brave New World of low- to medium-rise communities envisaged by the first generation of Labour politicians and planners. Their rather old-fashioned dream was to be replaced by a much more aggressive and modern approach to housing in the city. The Conservative Party returned to power in 1951 and pledged to increase house building to end the continuing housing crisis which the Labour Party had alleviated but not solved. Party politics was turning housing into a numbers game, and the easiest way to accommodate impressive numbers was to build higher and higher. Slum clearance, and the building of modern, high-density flats to replace the decaying Victorian tenements, was seen as the best way of meeting the needs of Central London. The great allies of the Conservative government in this mission were the LCC architects and planning departments where the young generation were strongly committed to the modern movement in architecture and the futuristic dream of a city in the sky.

Soon daringly modern projects began to change the skyline of London's Victorian suburbs. Blocks of flats were built higher than ever before, often reaching up between eight and twelve storeys. The 50s were the decade of great concrete slab blocks, both long and tall. The grandest project in this style in inner London was the Loughborough Road Estate in Brixton, built between 1954 and 1957. Most of its 1031 dwellings were maisonettes contained in eleven-storey slab blocks and these prototypes later became the standard model for the LCC's housing programme. These maisonettes were designed with coal fires, for central heating had not yet become a standard feature of council housing. This made life complicated both for the designers and the tenants. Coal had to be delivered in the lifts, the smoke from the fires was released through a system of flues, and the ash was disposed of through chutes or through the lift.

However, most tenants were to begin with very happy with their new flat life. The most popular feature of the flats was their generous room size, and the fact that each one contained a modern kitchen, bathroom and toilet. In addition, there was a positive response to high-rise living. The only serious survey of this in London was undertaken by sociologist Margaret Willis. She documented the remarkable fact that, after an initial period of anxiety, 90 per cent of families preferred to live on a high floor. Tenants preferred flats on higher levels because they were quieter. They often enjoyed spectacular views, too, and the air was more brac-

Publicity brochure for the Loughborough Road Estate in Brixton, built between 1954 and 1957. This daringly modern project was the prototype for many similar concrete slab blocks built by the LCC. To begin with, most residents actually preferred living on the upper storeys

ing. One of the first tenants to move onto the Loughborough Estate in 1956 was Pat Bloxham:

> When I moved up here it seemed strange to me – a great big place like this – and I really got scared. When I went outside I was terrified – I used to think that the walls were going to come away from me. When I was on the balcony, my legs just turned to jelly and I used to crawl to get inside again; it was terrifying. I wanted to run away. But after a while I got used to it and started to like it. My doctor told me if I lived up high it was better for your health – that's why I always used to be glad to be up high, to go out on the balcony and get all the fresh air. It was really lovely; you didn't want to go out anywhere, all you wanted to do was to stay up here in the sun and enjoy yourself. Oh, the views were beautiful! You look out and get Crystal Palace, the West End, you can see everywhere and everything; especially at night time when all the lights are on.

But by the late 1950s the building of new flats had almost ground to a halt. The grand plan had proved to be hugely expensive, principally due to the spiralling cost of land in the central areas which the post-war Labour government had shied away from nationalizing. And a series of cuts in housing grants by the new Conservative government meant that councils in poorer London areas had virtually no money to spend on their housing programmes and could offer little hope to local families looking for a council flat. In Islington the housing waiting-list was longer than almost anywhere else in London, and the council was forced to close it in 1957 when there were 16,000 families waiting for a new home.

The best chance of being rehoused was through the LCC but they too had an endless queue of poor families needing accommodation. The upshot of all this was that many people were living in slum conditions, confronted by a faceless bureaucracy which kept them waiting interminably for new homes. The anger and frustration that this generated exploded into many daily dramas in the LCC housing offices. Jim Cattle, who worked at Smithfield Market, had been on the council waiting-list for seven years:

> Their attitude was bombastic, dictatorial; it became a system of them and us. They had it, you wanted it, and they weren't going to give it to you. I used to be working from twelve o'clock at night and I'd come home about two in the afternoon, and instead of going to bed I'd go down to the LCC housing office

Jim and Dolly Cattle and their first daughter Rita, in 1951. They were one of thousands of families who waited many years on Islington Council's list of people to be rehoused

with Doll, the kids and all. It got to the point where we'd been down there about three or four times that week. We were talking to a geezer behind the ramp and it just clicked, wallop, like that. I just did my nut. I said, 'I want to see the Housing Manager and I want to see him now.' (You had more chance of visiting God than one of the Housing Managers.) I shall never forget it to this day – I jumped over the counter, I pushed the geezer out of the way, went up the corridor, kicked the door open, and there was the old Housing Manager sitting there. And I just blew my top.

Although the housing drive in inner London was slowing down, the Abercrombie plan to remove people and jobs to the new towns was now taking off. Government money was pumped into public housing schemes in new towns, like Stevenage in Hertfordshire and Harlow in Essex, which offered a great array of modern homes to Londoners wishing to begin a new life in the Home Counties. The only chance of a typical young couple getting a decent home in the late 1950s was for them to move away. And this was precisely what many thousands of families did.

This outward migration had been part of Abercrombie's plan for reducing overcrowding in Central London. But it was now taking an unpredicted and dangerous form. For the new towns were siphoning off just one type of person – the skilled worker and his family – and not a cross-section of the community as had originally been hoped. New towns were highly selective about whom they provided housing for, seeking to promote their image as magnets of skill and prosperity. To be eligible for a council house in a new town you had first to get a job and the firms moving out there normally only took their skilled workers with them. Thus the whole system of dispersal was heavily weighted in favour of the skilled working class. Families like the Cattles soon discovered that there was no hope of them ever getting a council home in a new town:

> When they started to build these new towns like Stevenage, they said, 'Well, would you like to go?' 'Yeh, cor, I'd love to go.' 'What do you do for a living?' Well, when I turned around and said to them I work at Smithfield Market they looked at me and said, 'Well, you'd better go back there.' We weren't qualified for anything like that. I'd have given my soul for a house, but you were just banging your head against a brick wall. I put my name down and all that and they took your particulars, and that's as far as you ever got. Most people that went to these New Towns were skilled people – mechanics, tool setters, and so on. After all, it was a new town being built out of the rubble and they wanted the craftsmen to go with it; they wanted the industries, they didn't want Tom, Dick and Harry going down there to take up the properties. So with me not being skilled we had no chance, no chance at all.

Abercrombie's plan meant that in Central London an excess of people who were semi-skilled, unskilled, old and sick were left behind. The future life blood of the old balanced community was being drained away. Neither had the plan made allowance for a lot of people moving into the city to replace those who had moved out. From the mid-1950s onwards many thousands entered run-down inner London boroughs like Islington. Some were Commonwealth immigrants attracted by cheap rented housing; but there was also another type of newcomer. That was the pioneer middle-class gentrifier who was buying up and restoring some of the old houses that were being sold off cheaply. Just when the working classes were escaping from their tenement past, so their social superiors were rediscovering the beauty of the bug-infested buildings that had for generations housed the poor.

Canonbury was one of the first parts of London to be gentrified and many of those who moved into its elegant Georgian town houses were young architects like Harley Sherlock:

> We wanted to be in the centre of things, we wanted to be where everybody was, we wanted a change from suburbia which wasn't where life was going on, we wanted to be part of London; we wanted to be where working people of all sorts were, and all this we found in Canonbury. In those days properties in Central London were cheap, nobody wanted to live in the centre. We bought two very nice buildings and each house I

Canonbury was one of the first parts of London to be gentrified

Below: Many of the pioneer gentrifiers were young architects, like Harley Sherlock (right), who moved here with five architect friends in 1952

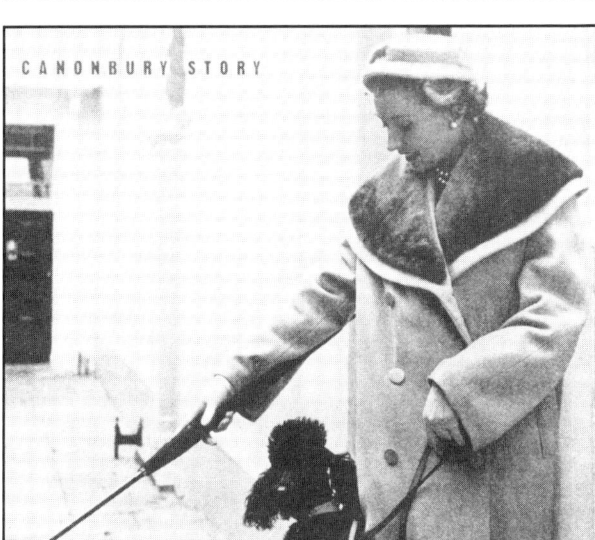

Above left: These Georgian houses were bought for £2650 apiece in the early 50s. Parked outside are the 'vintage' second-hand cars of the new Bohemian residents

think cost us £2650 which by today's standards is just ridiculous. Most people wanted to live in the leafy suburbs; indeed, my parents thought I was mad to come and live in dirty, grubby old London. But for those of us who were young and wanted to do something different, this was an absolutely marvellous opportunity. We were a sort of co-operative of young idealistic architects and we wanted to join the two houses we'd bought together. So we held a sort of house-warming party, we gave the guests pickaxes and crowbars, and we showed them where to make a hole from one house into the other, one at first floor level and one in the basement. And we offered a prize of a bottle of Schnapps for the first person to get through. This turned out to be very hard work in the basement because it was an

Left: A photograph from a feature on Canonbury in *Good Housekeeping* in 1953. By this time Canonbury was beginning to take off as a fashionable residential area

> eighteen-inch thick brick wall, which was rather thicker than we'd expected, but it certainly was a good party. I think Canonbury started to become fashionable because it had a lot of very beautiful grand houses and people were getting tired of commuting into London every day. And, of course, there were articles being published at the time drawing attention to the fact that more and more people (I suppose they'd be called trendy people now), were hitting on the idea of moving into Central London. *Good Housekeeping* magazine did a sort of article with fashion models standing on the steps of various pretty houses in Canonbury. It mentioned that five young architects and furniture designers had moved into the area. That was us.

Cleaner air in Central London helped to promote even more gentrification in once beautiful areas like Canonbury, Camden and Clapham. Until the mid-1950s one fact which had always made people in the suburbs think twice about moving to an inner area was the dreadful 'pea souper' smogs which engulfed Central London every winter. The smogs reduced visibility in inner areas to a few inches and coated Londoners with a thin layer of dirt and dust. They also helped to cause many deaths every year by heightening breathing problems amongst the young and the very old. However, the Clean Air Act which introduced rigorous smoke controls in Central London from the late 1950s onwards brought to an end the era of the 'pea souper'.

London smog scenes of the early 50s. The Clean Air Act brought to an end the era of the 'pea souper', and encouraged even more gentrification in once beautiful areas like Canonbury and Camden

Gentrification was further promoted because traffic congestion was making commuting and long journeys to work increasingly difficult. There was a growing realization by the middle-class younger generation that it was better to live close to work in Central London than to commute hundreds of miles a week as their parents had done.

By the early 1960s the movement of architects and media professionals back into Islington was increasing rapidly. As Canonbury filled up, so the newcomers discovered Barnsbury, and set about transforming one of the worst slums in London into a splendid period suburb. House-hunting young couples became experts at spotting the up-and-coming areas. They looked for sand and cement mixers on the pavement – tell-tale signs of renovation. And, most important, they noted how many houses in a street possessed brass door knockers and were painted white. This was the badge of the pioneer and to outsiders it announced that there was a gentrifier within determined to restore the house to its original glory.

This colonization of areas like Barnsbury by middle-class pioneers began to bring a new atmosphere and culture to wedges of inner London. Through the newly formed Barnsbury Society, the gentrifiers pursued imaginative schemes for tree-plantings, street furniture replacement and traffic control, all of which helped to restore the charm of the area's Georgian squares and terraces. The dominant style of the gentrifiers was one of elegant austerity, or what has been called 'conspicuous thrift'. Many had been rebellious students and they rejected the brash materialism and showiness of the affluent society in favour of a natural and unpretentious look. Their furniture was stripped pine; their walls were painted white rather than papered; and their floorboards were sanded to remove the varnish then left uncovered. An indication of the changing character of Barnsbury can be seen in the census figures; the proportion of men employed in managerial and professional jobs rose from 3 per cent in 1961 to over 15 per cent ten years later.

The social character of Islington in the early 1960s was fairly typical of London's inner boroughs. They contained three main kinds of housing and lifestyle. First, there were the up-and-coming areas, where a few thousand pioneer gentrifiers were busy restoring the Georgian houses and squares. Second, there were dozens of council estates on which families enjoyed the comforts and convenience of living in modern flats. Third came the thousands of privately rented flats, in which the great majority still lived. Slum clearance had only scratched the surface of London's housing problems. And amongst this new poor there was a growing proportion of old, sick, immigrant and unskilled people.

What led to the rediscovery of these appalling conditions was the Profumo sex scandal of 1963. The revelations about Defence Minister Profumo's illicit sex life threw up another name, that of Peter Rachman, who had also been involved with the two women at the centre of the scandal, Christine Keeler and Mandy Rice-Davies. The press took advantage of the fact that Rachman had died the year before to expose his rise to power as London's richest slum landlord. He had arrived in London in 1946 a penniless and stateless refugee having survived a German concentration camp in his native Poland. He moved into the property business, buying up run-down houses after a prostitute girl friend lent him the money to start a flat-letting agency. Within a few years he had built up a huge empire of seedy and crumbling properties, most of them in the then unfashionable Notting Hill area. By intimidating tenants, sometimes taking fierce alsatian dogs round to their doors, he replaced unprofitable white tenants with West Indians, who were desperate for accommodation at any price and were willing to put up with terrible overcrowding.

The Rachman exposé led to a government investigation being set in motion to probe into housing conditions in the capital. In 1964 it produced the Milner-Holland report which revealed the housing horrors of inner London. Islington was pinpointed as one of the worst areas, for it had fewer basic facilities than anywhere else in the capital. Most of its households still did not have exclusive use of running water, a bath or a toilet. It also had the largest number of overcrowded households in London. The horrors of living in what was increasingly being called 'the inner city' began to be highlighted in a number of television documentaries and popular films, the most influential of which was *Cathy Come Home*. It featured the plight of a homeless woman and her children, and

Washing up in a tenement slum in Poplar in the early 60s. The housing horrors of inner London were rediscovered at this time

was the decade's most powerful statement about appalling housing conditions in London: appropriately it was filmed for the most part in Islington.

Out of painful revelations like these was to emerge a new dream of banishing bad housing and poverty from London. The Abercrombie plan had failed but a second great wave of planning and social engineering was to begin in the mid-1960s. It was to be even more influential than the one which followed the war.

This new concern about the inner city coincided with two momentous changes. First came the reform of London's government in 1963: the boundaries drawn up for the new GLC doubled the geographical size of the old LCC which it replaced. Then the Labour Party returned to power. They captured control of the GLC and returned to national office in 1964 for the first time in thirteen years. There was a new determination to banish tenement poverty in the Victorian ghettos of inner London forever.

For example, attempts were made to move people out from poor, overcrowded inner boroughs like Islington into the leafy suburbs of towns like Bromley in Kent which were now part of the GLC. Evelyn Dennington, first Chairperson of the Housing Committee, led this crusade to get families out of the slums of inner London. However, the Conservative outer boroughs were eager to maintain their exclusive character and open spaces. They refused to co-operate with the plan and used stalling tactics to prevent any mass movement out of inner London and by 1965 it was clear that this strategy had failed. Next came the building of a second generation of new towns. Milton Keynes, Peterborough and Northampton were designated as London's overspill new towns. Milton Keynes was planned like a mini Los Angeles with the most advanced house designs and every conceivable facility. But this was a long-term solution. The time that had to be spent on planning and building the new grid system at Milton Keynes meant it would be several years before people were able to move out there.

A short-term radical solution to the problem of bad housing was needed, and in the mid-1960s it was seen to be the tower block. Politicians, planners and architects all agreed that high-rise flat building was the best way to provide housing that was cheap, quick and attractive. This was not an unreasonable assumption given the popularity and success of flats built in the 1950s. The heart of this new vision of the City Beautiful was the system-built tower block. Basically, the idea was to stand the street on its end, pointing up into the sky, in order to save space. These tall, slim blocks, some of them twenty-four storeys high, were to be made in factories, then erected on the site, thus saving time and money in the strife-torn building industry. In 1965 the Labour government passed new legislation which provided generous grants for a glut of slum clearance and high-rise building programmes. It forced councils like Islington to use system-building in order to improve their housing record. The Victorian slums of the past were to be bulldozed to make way for the tower blocks of the future.

To begin with, these new tower blocks and system building appeared to provide the answer to the problems of the inner city. In 1967 the number of new homes completed in London soared. Islington, which had expanded its boundaries to include what had previously been Finsbury as part of the new GLC re-organization, was much more cautious about tower blocks than most other boroughs, but it still achieved record levels of rehousing through system building. The 400 high-rise blocks which sprouted up in

Lord Mountbatten opens a new GLC tower block in 1966. High-rise flats were seen as the solution to bad housing in the 60s. More than 400 were built in the capital

London in the late 1960s were opened with municipal splendour, some of them winning prizes for their design and architecture. The East End borough of Newham demolished great swathes of prefabs and Victorian terraces to build 125 of them, more than anywhere else in London.

But very quickly the high-rise dream went wrong. It soon became clear that many Londoners hated living in the new tower blocks. Politicians and planners who commissioned them had been seduced by a numbers game which gave impressive rehousing figures but created untold human misery. However, this rejection of high rise was not as simple and uniform as we now often imagine. The luxurious and spacious interiors of the flats were welcomed, especially by those who had just escaped from tenement slums. Some towers, which were well designed and enjoyed strong tenants' associations and good caretakers, were very popular amongst residents. But there were two serious grievances that quickly turned many tenants against the tower blocks. The first concerned the lifts, which were too few, too small and too slow. Worst of all they were constantly breaking down and could easily be vandalised. And because of a shortage of money for back-up, the tiny management and maintenance staff of the GLC often took a long time to put things right. This hadn't been a problem in the flats built in the 1950s, which were generally much lower and often had stairs as opposed to lifts. Lift break-downs meant that those living on the upper levels faced exhausting journeys up and down hundreds of stairs to get in and out. For the old, the sick and mothers with young children, these long climbs were an appalling prospect. The break-downs resulted in some people being stranded for hours or occasionally days. Doreen Reid lived on one of the top floors of a high-rise block in Plaistow with her husband and baby Tracy in the late 1960s:

> The first problem I discovered was the lifts; that was the first nasty experience. I had a rather large pram for Tracy when she was a baby. I went out one day and I came back and my lift wasn't working. Well, I had twenty-four flights of stairs to get up to my flat. It was very, very hard work and took me ages. I had visions of Tracy coming out of the pram, my shopping going everywhere and I didn't attempt it again after that. So if the lift wasn't working then I just couldn't go out at all. I was virtually in the flat all the time until the lift was going. Sometimes it would take a day, sometimes two days, and I just couldn't get out at all because to take baby out in the pram was impossible.

The second grievance came specifically from families with

young children, who found the tower blocks totally unsuited to their needs. Lack of play space for children inside and outside the towers created a claustrophobic atmosphere. It was impossible to supervise children's outdoor play and mothers were terrified at the prospect of their children falling off balconies, out of windows, or downstairs. Doreen Reid:

> There was virtually nowhere for Tracy, or any other child, to play. Our block was on a main road, so you had the traffic down there. The only place she could play basically was in her bedroom or the lounge area. The only time I could open the balcony door was if I was in the room with her continually because with young children, when they're growing up, they're into everything. I couldn't let her out – but I got neighbours complaining if she made too much noise indoors, like the tenant underneath or the tenant upstairs. I remember one day I was out in the kitchen doing some hand-washing, and I thought to myself 'Tracy's quiet, what's she up to?' And I called out to her and I got no answer. I thought, 'That's not like her.' I wandered into the lounge and it was then I realized that the balcony door was open, and I thought 'Oh no!' I just went cold, literally cold; I stepped out onto the balcony, and I instinctively looked over the top because I fully expected to find Tracy at the bottom. When I looked down and found she wasn't there I came in and I looked in my bedroom first; she wasn't there, and then I went into her bedroom and there she was playing with her toys. But at the time it gave me a very very bad fright.

But what really brought the brief heyday of the tower block to an end was its terrible structural defects. Some of the towers were inadequately tested and built to unsafe heights. In 1968 disaster struck when Ronan Point, a brand new block of system-built flats in Newham, partially collapsed, killing five people. This tragedy, combined with the growing chorus of complaints from residents, created an increasing crisis of confidence in the tower block. After Ronan Point, the GLC didn't commission any more tower blocks, though because contracts had already been signed with builders and because they took several years to complete, new and in a sense unwanted towers continued to appear until the 1970s. By this time, however, the GLC had turned to lower rise estates and more traditional designs for its building programmes.

Now, a new policy came to replace tower block building: the 're-hab'. Instead of knocking down Georgian and Victorian buildings in the inner city, they were to be renovated and given a new

In 1968 Ronan Point tower block in Newham collapsed, killing five people. This tragedy brought the brief heyday of the tower block to an end

lease of life. The Labour Party's 1969 Housing Bill offered generous improvement grants to whoever owned these properties, especially in areas like Islington where there was a lot of old poor housing. The turn-around was ironic, for only a few years earlier many old areas worthy of restoration were condemned and bulldozed in the clean-sweep planning phase of the mid-1960s. The most notorious planning blunder in Islington was the razing of the Packington Estate, a picturesque neighbourhood of Georgian terraces and squares close to the Angel tube station. Despite a strong protest movement by local tenants and the fact that the proposed new estate could cost millions more than a restoration programme, the old Packington bit the dust. It was somehow appropriate, however, that the Labour Party should have turned its back on the tower block in 1969, for that year was its last in office and it marked the end of the second great wave of idealism and social engineering in London's post-war history.

'Re-hab' and home improvement grants were originally intended to improve the housing standards of the poorer people living in inner-city areas. In fact, they were to give a great impetus to the removal of the original tenants and to more gentrification by middle-class newcomers. By the early 1970s there was a huge demand amongst professional people for old houses conveniently situated in Central London that they could restore and renovate with the help of a home improvement grant. The old and hard-up home-owners in places like Islington suddenly found they were sitting on a gold mine and they sold their run-down houses to young middle-class couples for what they thought were huge sums. In 1970 an early Victorian terraced house with three storeys would fetch around £5000. They then moved out to places like Romford and Ilford in Essex on the proceeds.

Landlords, estate agents and property developers were, however, far more important than home-owners in exploiting this market for gentrification. They were ruthless in wheedling out their tenants, for to offer vacant possession of a house added thousands to the price it could fetch on the market. Some landlords locked tenants out of their lavatories, switched off the gas and electricity, smashed their windows and hired thugs in suits to harass or beat up residents. Some reported their properties to the local council as being unfit for habitation and demanded that their tenants be rehoused. Others offered cash bribes – usually £200 for eviction – which some tenants, totally ignorant of their rights, eagerly accepted. But, while home owners were often eager to sell their houses, many private tenants wanted to stay as they had nowhere to go. The stage was set for many hundreds of bitter feuds between tenants and landlords.

In one street in Barnsbury, this conflict flared up into what became known as 'the Battle of Stonefield Street'. Stonefield Street contained some very attractive but run-down Georgian houses and, from the late 1960s onwards, landlords, in league with property developers, had started winkling out and buying off the tenants one by one. To encourage others to go, landlords stopped doing basic repairs to homes. But there remained a hard core of tenants who refused to move. There was fierce resistance because this was one of the few streets where the old working-class community remained very much intact. Ray Spreadbury, a baker, had lived in the street since just after the war:

> The actual words of the estate agents were 'Barnsbury is a chicken fit for plucking', meaning that they could wheedle and winkle tenants out and sell the houses to the gentry who wanted to move in. You see, the area's close to the City of London and it's also close to the West End – an ideal spot what with houses going cheap. Of course, we thought we'd got to do something about it, because we were a community in this street. There were all kinds of tradesmen living here; there were market tradesmen, bricklayers, carpenters, bakers; you name it, we had it in this street, and everybody knew everybody else. And if you wanted a job done you just sent to a particular chap. Anything you wanted you could get done even our car repairs. Of course we were a bit reluctant to lose a community like that. So we decided that it was time to have a meeting and we met in a house round the square. I thought to myself, 'Well, the only way we can beat these people is to form ourselves into some kind of community group to really get down to it; so this is what we did. I was the one who was to be the chairman.

The tenants' association held meetings each week to campaign against bribery and harassment. The battle was to reach its climax one day in September 1973, as Ray Spreadbury recalls:

> People were being harassed by these winklers and especially people like Mrs Murphy who lived in number sixteen. I came along one day from work and there were workmen actually knocking her front wall down and her house was open. I knew that Mrs Murphy and her husband were both at work, and I knew she wouldn't have given them permission to knock her house down just like that. They looked like cowboys. So I thought the best thing to do was to get in touch with James Pitt at the Housing Centre and get a solicitor on the job, to get an injunction and stop the work. That was what we did.

When Eileen Murphy came home from work she had a terrible shock:

> There was scaffolding up and they'd pulled all the wall down.

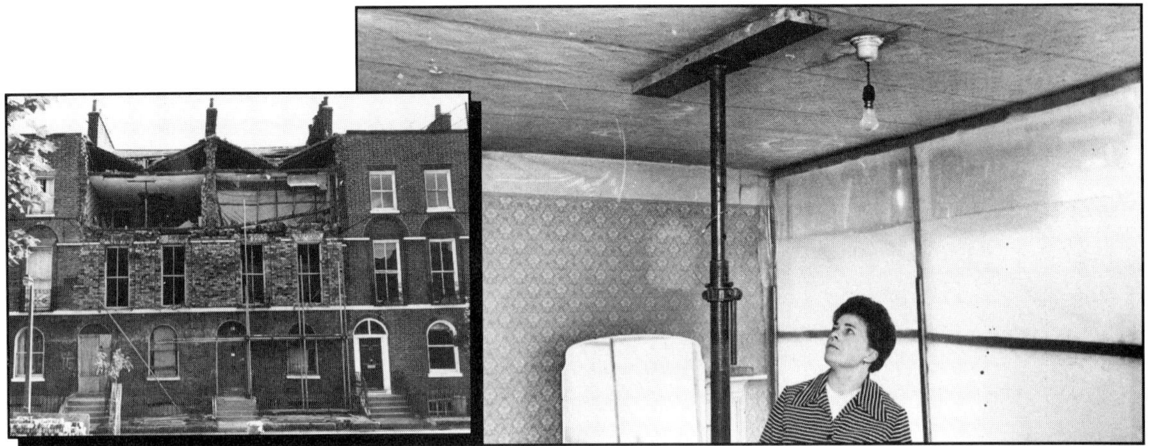

Above: The wall of Eileen Murphy's home at 16 Stonefield Street, Islington, was demolished by unscrupulous developers in September 1973, in order to force her to move out

Above right: Eileen Murphy inspects the clamp stuck between her ceiling and her bed. This was the most violent case of harassment in what came to be known as the Battle of Stonefield Street

There were these great big men standing there with pickaxes, and things like that; well, I just didn't know what to do. There were bricks and mortar all over the place, and no cover to stop it getting through to the rest of the house. I went upstairs and there was this big scaffolding thing stuck on the bed with a note, a nasty note stuck to the ceiling, saying 'you dirty B'. I was really frightened because the house was all open at the front and anyone could get in. I didn't want to be pushed out, you see. I'd been there twenty-one years, and I didn't think I was of an age to be moved around. I didn't know what to do, I was scared. Then Mr Spreadbury came along and the neighbourhood lawyer James Pitt and Mr Cunningham, who was the MP for Islington.

In the legal battle which followed, the development company Preebles, who were responsible for demolishing Mrs Murphy's walls, lost their case, and Islington Council were able to purchase and renovate much of Stonefield Street for the original tenants. The victory was a result of the strength of the old Stonefield Street community. But, because Islington's communities had been weakened so much in the previous decades, victories like this were rare. Most of Islington's desirable streets were gradually emptied of their original tenants to make way for gentrifiers arriving from the outer suburbs, the Home Counties, or even further afield.

The 1970s were a boom time for gentrification. Battles, similar to those in Islington, were fought across the whole of Central London, as a new generation of pioneers moved in to Georgian and Victorian streets and squares in places like Battersea, Brixton, Camden, Camberwell and Clapham. But by now the enterprise of gentrification was changing in character – it was becoming highly fashionable. The austere look, which had always been the hallmark of the gentrifier, was increasingly becoming an expensive style in itself. To service the fashionable gentrifiers' needs, a new inner-city economy of 'up-market' small businesses and craftsmen's shops mushroomed. Shops selling antiques, furniture and old books, delicatessens, health food stores, wine bars and bistros, all became familiar monuments to the new affluent lifestyle. Old, semi-derelict shopping arcades like Camden Passage in Islington were transformed into busy and pricey emporiums for the gentrifiers. The money that fuelled this refurbishing of the inner city came from London's booming office economy and from the expansion in the media and the arts in the capital. And, as it became more and more fashionable to live in this stripped-pine belt in Central London, so house and flat prices soared to astronomical heights. The average cost of a house in Islington, for example, rose from around £6000 in the mid-1960s, to £30,000 in the mid-1970s, to £150,000 by the mid-1980s. What had begun as a rather bohemian movement, often pioneered by men and women who were rejecting the suburban comforts and class snobbery of their parents' generation, had turned full circle. Increasingly, it was only the rich who could afford to buy a house in a well-established, fashionable area like Barnsbury or Canonbury.

But while the 1970s saw the world of the gentrifiers become more and more expensive and exclusive, the majority of their neighbours became worse off. This helped to create a stark contrast between the new rich and the new poor in the inner city. Many commentators observed a deterioration in the quality of working-class life in inner London, and one explanation for this was the gradual disintegration of the old communities that used to live there. It would be unfair to pin too much blame for any social disintegration that has occurred on the planning disasters of the post-war years. However, there is no doubt that by the 1970s they were partly responsible for the escalation of social problems like crime. Essentially, the new estates that by then dominated the landscape of inner London helped to undermine the old community and family network that once bound together working-class neighbourhoods. In the old terraces of Islington and Bethnal Green people had struck up friendships with neighbours by talking in the garden, in the street or in the corner shop. Doreen Reid recalls:

> Where I used to live, everybody knew everybody in the street. You'd see your neighbour each day out in the garden; you'd have the odd cup of tea; either I'd make it or my neighbour

> would make it, and there'd always be something going on. We'd either be talking about the gardens or the children, or the dogs or whatever, but it was totally different when I moved into a tower block. There were about sixty families in it, but you might just as well have lived on your own because once you shut your street door you were on your own, you had no one to talk to. You felt like a prisoner.

Parents and grandparents had informally kept an eye on children and young people. This helped to contain and control the kind of serious crime and violence which flared up in the 1970s. But the new estates, where flats were much more isolated and surrounded by dark corridors, in a sense invited delinquency with their basement car parks, pedestrian tunnels and landscaped gardens, which were out of sight of adults and which quickly became night-time no-go areas of vandalism and violence. There were often few facilities like the traditional street-corner shop, pub or club, which in the past had been the engines of the local community.

At the heart of the old communities of inner London had been a great web of family and kinship links – and this too was to be inadvertently punctured by the grand plans of the post-war years. In their classic sociological study, *Family and Kinship in East London*, Michael Young and Peter Wilmott have documented an incredibly close and caring community which used to exist in the terraced rows of Bethnal Green in the 1950s. Practically all married daughters lived within a stone's throw of their mothers, with the result that some grandmothers might have sixty or so relatives living in their neighbourhood. But by the 1970s two generations of migration to new towns, to out-country estates and to high-rise developments scattered all over London, had seriously undermined this kind of inner-city community. Despite the iniquities of the old private rented system, landlords had at least often been responsive to mothers trying to get flats in the neighbourhood for their married daughters. Their new municipal landlords fared very badly on this score, and many families were broken up by council bureaucracies which made little effort to offer local accommodation to sons and daughters. The main cost was to be paid by the older people who were left behind. Many were lonely, isolated and lived in fear of crime. And increasingly they came to depend on the state for basic services that might once have been provided by their families. The experience of the Cattle family in Islington vividly illustrates how the older generation were becoming stranded in the inner city:

> We desperately wanted our two daughters to live close to us here in a council home in Islington, and they desperately wanted to as well. We had a big battle with the council over this and they said there was no chance. I remember when my daughter had been on the housing list for four years and I went down and asked, 'Why is she being pushed aside like this?' He said, 'How long have you lived in the borough?' So I said, 'My family goes back six generations in this borough.' He said, 'Well, it's about time you moved over then and gave somebody else a chance.' Both my daughters have been forced to move out, one to Brighton and the other to South London. It was heart-breaking and we don't see each other or the grandchildren as often as we want. The reason it happened was because of the huge waiting-list, and gentrification as well has made it more difficult to find homes for our children. What has happened is that the old Islington community had been broken up. We've lived here for six generations and so have a lot of people like us but we're the last in the line now, we're the last generation. Islington's been taken over; we say it's been raped. When we look at the old people we see ourselves in a few years' time: isolated and dependent on authority and beholden to local government.

Most demoralizing to those forced to live on the new estates was their rapid physical decay in the 1970s. The transformation from showcase to sink estate in many cases took only several years, and appalling structural problems began to emerge. Walls and roofs leaked, drains became easily blocked and heating systems broke down. Often weeks or months passed before they were repaired. Most bizarre of all, some estates in Hackney began to be plagued by Pharaoh ants, a tropical species of brown insect that was attracted to the warm-air ducts of their central-heating systems. As local councils spent millions patching up the concrete and glass dinosaurs they were saddled with, and as the poor tenants prepared to live with the consequences of the planning disasters, there was a great debate as to who was responsible for this catastrophe. In the ensuing legal battles for compensation the finger was pointed at unscrupulous builders and manufacturers, incompetent architects, politicians and councillors greedy for votes, and at planners who knew little or nothing about the building industry. But, remarkably, nobody was found accountable.

At the root of the social problems and the growing inequality in the inner city, however, was the decline of its traditional manufacturing industry. As a result of the recession many factories went to the wall or moved out to green-field sites to avoid high rents and traffic congestion. The effect was a relative decline in wage levels, an increase in job insecurity and, most important, mass unemployment which by the 1980s had increased to around 20 per cent in London's inner city boroughs. In Islington the death of the clothing, furniture and precision metal factories fuelled an increase in unemployment from 500 in 1954 to 3000 in 1974 to 17,000 in 1982. Poverty and unemployment had devastating social consequences, not least of which was their contribution to the increase in crime in the inner city. Unemployment, irregular wages and low pay were concentrated amongst the young, especially young blacks – and so was crime. Having no job or no job worth having, they turned to mugging, burglary, violence and vandalism as a way of getting money and excitement.

Planners and politicians could not be blamed for the decline of manufacturing industry in inner London. The eclipse of London, position as the workshop of the world had deep structural causes, as we saw in Chapter One. However, the plan to export people and jobs away from inner London to the new towns, conceived by Abercrombie and enshrined in government policy for thirty years, did undoubtedly drain away some of the capital's remaining wealth and economic vitality. By 1976 Abercrombie's plan to reduce the population of Greater London seemed to be getting out of hand. The population was by then down to 7 million and there were fears that the continual movement out was crippling the capital by creaming off all the best industries and skilled workers.

It was in recognition of this that from 1976 onwards the GLC began fiercely to oppose further new town development, viewing it as a serious threat to London's future. By this time the government had switched its investment programmes from new towns to inner-city renewal and regeneration. Public money was increasingly spent on improving housing and education in the inner city, and on trying to attract industry back into London. These kinds of initiatives were broadened from 1981 onwards when the Labour Party won control of the GLC. Led by Ken Livingstone, the GLC began a crusade to revitalize London's industries through the creation of GLEB (the Greater London Enterprise Board), and it channelled considerable resources into improving the position of disadvantaged minority and racial groups in the inner city. However, the problems that were being tackled ran so deep that despite the creation of jobs and improved facilities, the inner city remained in a state of crisis.

It was in this context that the third post-war dream of a new and better world emerged. This was the dream of Thatcherism which was put into practice in the 1980s after the Conservative Party returned to office in 1979 led by Margaret Thatcher. It was a very different dream to those which had preceded it, for whereas two generations of social engineers had attacked what was seen as the evil legacy of London's Victorian past, the new dream tried to resurrect the glories of this same past, through the restoration of Victorian values. Good housekeeping, free interprise and discipline were seen as the cure for the ailing inner city.

The effect was to summon up London's Victorian past, but it was an uglier past than most people had imagined. In practice, the belief in good housekeeping meant harsh cuts in money for housing. The little money that was available was spent on patching up the high-rise blocks; new council-house building in London ground to a virtual standstill. And the policy of selling council properties as a way of raising cash and transforming disillusioned council tenants into proud home-owners has met with little success in the inner city. Most of the housing stock is high rise, and the great majority of tenants dislike their flats so intensely that they have no desire to buy them. The housing crisis in the inner city and the problem of homelessness is as much of an issue in the 1980s as it ever was in Victorian times.

The belief in free enterprise has created some new jobs in inner-city areas like Islington, but they have mostly been in the sweated trades which have flourished as controls on pay and conditions have been relaxed. Asian and Cypriot workers – many of them women working at home – spend long hours toiling at sewing machines, churning out shirts, jackets and coats, to be paid at wages as low as thirty pence an hour. They do this in the 1980s because they have to in order to survive – just as their Victorian forebears, the Jewish immigrants, had to. Conditions in the sweatshops hark back strongly to those days.

The belief in discipline has resulted not in higher standards of behaviour but a strengthening of the forces of law and order to deal with the growing threat to life in London. There are some parallels between present-day vilence and the Victorian experience. In 1886 the West End was in a state of siege as a huge and violent crowd of unemployed labourers attacked the rich and looted from expensive shop windows. There were fears of a revolution. In that same year the LCC was formed, and it turned into a powerful instrument for the improvement of education, health and housing in the capital. It is a sad indictment of a hundred years of London history that after a century of attempts to build a better life in the capital, the Metropolitan Police are in 1986 busy arming themselves for riots on a far greater scale than anything that happened in 1886. The fact that the GLC, heir to the LCC, was in 1986 scrapped by Mrs Thatcher's government was indicative of a new prevailing mood of disillusionment with planning and social reform. Radical LCC leaders had often fallen foul of central government, creating mutual suspicion and antagonism, but there had always been a commitment to the idea of a London-wide local state. With the advent of Thatcherism, however, the old consensus on democratic social reform broke down. The new government's astonishing way of combating the socialist policies of the GLC under Ken Livingstone was simply to end its existence.

What all this means for the future of London is a matter of much conjecture. Mrs Thatcher's government has had an immense impact on the capital, but it will be replaced sooner or later, and a new government may well revive something similar to the GLC. The workings of a metropolis the size of London are so complex that in the long run it will probably demand a London-wide government in order to function more smoothly and democratically. At the heart of London's future, however, is the success or failure of its economy and, despite serious problems, its prospects are not quite so gloomy as they appear at first sight. Although its manufacturing industry is likely to decline even more, and the drift of people and jobs out of the capital into the South East is likely to continue, some key sections of London's economy are prospering and growing. Central London still possesses a thriving office economy of banks and insurance companies, tourism is booming and London remains one of the world's leading style capitals. London thus continues to create enormous wealth, just as it did in Victorian times. But one huge problem which remains unresolved is how this wealth is made and how it should be shared. For, despite the fact that the standard of living of all Londoners has improved greatly since the days of nineteenth-century social investigators like Charles Booth and Henry Mayhew, the stark inequalities between the classes and between the rich and the poor remain. This class division in the capital has been one of the main threads in the story of the making of modern London, helping to shape its social life, its social geography and its politics. It also promises to play an important role in the capital's future.

Further Reading

Of the many books we have read, the following were particularly interesting and informative:

Chapter 1: Greater London Council, *London Industrial Strategy* (GLC 1985), *The West London Report* (GLC 1985), *The East London Report* (GLC 1984), *Multinationals: Special Report* (GLC 1984), R. Douglas Brown, *The Port of London* (Lavenham Press 1978), Antony Hugill, *Sugar And All That: A History of Tate and Lyle* (Gentry Books 1978), and Arthur Marwick, *British Society Since 1945* (Penguin 1982).

Chapter 2: John Platt, *London Rock Routes* (Fourth Estate 1985), Richard Barnes, *Mods!* (Eel Pie Publishing 1979), George Melly, *Revolt into Style: The Pop Arts in Britain* (Penguin 1970), Francis Wheen, *The Sixties* (Century Publishing 1982), Jonathan Aitken, *The Young Meteors* (Secker and Warburg 1967), Iain Chambers, *Urban Rhythms: Pop Music and Popular Culture* (Macmillan 1985), S. Hall and T. Jefferson (eds.) *Resistance Through Rituals* (Hutchinson 1976), and Jeffrey Weeks, *Sex, Politics and Society: The Regulation of Sexuality Since 1800* (Longman 1981).

Chapter 3: Oliver Marriott, *The Property Boom*, (Hamish Hamilton 1967), P. Daniels, *Office Location: An Urban and Regional Study* (G. Bell and Sons 1975), P. Daniels, *Service Industries: A Geographical Appraisal* (Methuen 1985), Rosemary Crompton and Gareth Jones, *White Collar Proletariat: Deskilling and Gender in Clerical Work* (Macmillan 1984), John Plender and Paul Wallace, *The Square Mile* (Century Hutchinson 1985), Alan Delgado, *The Enormous File: A Social History of the Office* (John Murray 1979), Oliver Leigh Wood, *From Splendour to Banality: The Rebuilding of the City of London 1945-1983* (SAVE Britain's Heritage 1983), Geoffrey Ingham, *Capitalism Divided? The City and Industry in British Social Development* (Macmillan 1984), Kenneth Hudson and Julian Pettifer, *Diamonds in the Sky: A Social History of Air Travel* (Bodley Head 1979), Peter Cowan, *The Office: A Facet of Urban Growth* (Heinemann 1969), Jack Rose, *The Dynamics of Urban Property Development* (E. and F. Spon, 1985).

Chapter 4: Peter Hall, *The Containment of Urban England* (2 Vols.) (Allen and Unwin 1973), David Thomas, *London's Green Belt* (Faber and Faber 1970), Ray Thomas, *London's New Towns:*

A Study of Self Contained and Balanced Communities (PEP 1969), Howard Newby, *Green and Pleasant Land? Social Change in Rural England* (Hutchinson 1979), Harold Orlans, *Stevenage: A Sociological Study of A New Town* (Routledge and Kegan Paul 1952), and John Connell, *The End of Tradition: Country Life in Central Surrey* (Routledge and Kegan Paul 1978).

Chapter 5: Peter Fryer, *Staying Power: The History of Black People in Britain* (Pluto 1984), Dilip Hiro, *Black British, White British* (Pelican 1973), Trevor Lee, *Race and Residence: The Concentration and Dispersal of Immigrants in London* (Clarendon Press 1977), James Walvin, *Passage to Britain: Immigration in British History and Politics* (Penguin 1984), The Open University, *Ethnic Minorities and Community Relations Course, Units 8-9 Minority Experience* (Open University 1982), James Watson, *Between Two Cultures* (Blackwell 1977), Sheila Patterson, *Dark Strangers* (Tavistock Publications 1963), and Ruth Glass, *Newcomers* (Allen and Unwin 1960).

Chapter 6: Paul Harrison, *Inside The Inner City* (Penguin 1983), Lionel Esher, *A Broken Wave: The Rebuilding of England 1940-1980* (Allen Lane 1981), Alison Ravetz, *Re-Making Cities* (Croom Helm 1980), Jonathan Raban, *Soft City* (Hamish Hamilton 1974), Paul Addison, *Now The War Is Over: A Social History Of Britain 1945-51* (BBC 1985), Nicholas Deakin and Clare Ungerson, *Leaving London: Planned Mobility and the Inner City* (Heinemann 1977), Michael Young and Peter Willmott, *Family and Kinship in East London* (Penguin 1979), Ken Young and John Kramer, *Strategy and Conflict in Metropolitan Housing* (Heinemann 1978), and Ken Young and Patricia Garside, *Metropolitan London: Politics and Urban Change 1837-1981* (Edward Arnold 1982).

A number of the areas which this book explores are only thinly documented and much interesting and important information can be obtained by tapping people's memories. For advice on how to go about this see Steve Humphries, *The Handbook of Oral History* (Inter-Action 1984) or contact the London History Workshop Centre who arrange workshops on tape recording oral history. They also hold the complete archive of the four series and books of *The Making of Modern London* which contains many taped interviews, letters and photographs. If you wish to have access to this material contact them at: 42 Queen Square, London WC1 3AJ

Index